PSYCHODOODLES

A selection of John C. Holden's surreal prints
patterned for the adult colorist

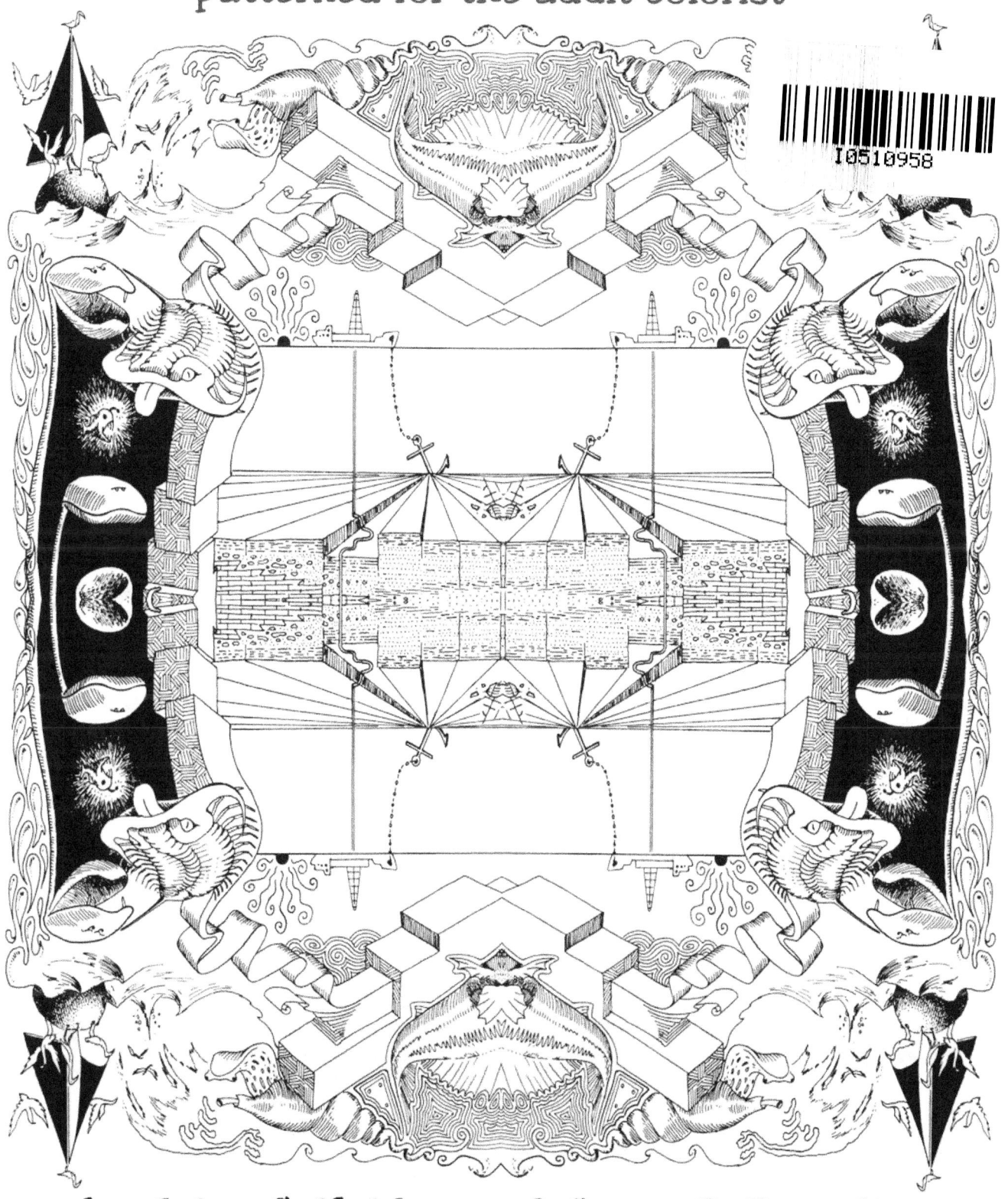

by John C. Holden and Gregg R. Brandly

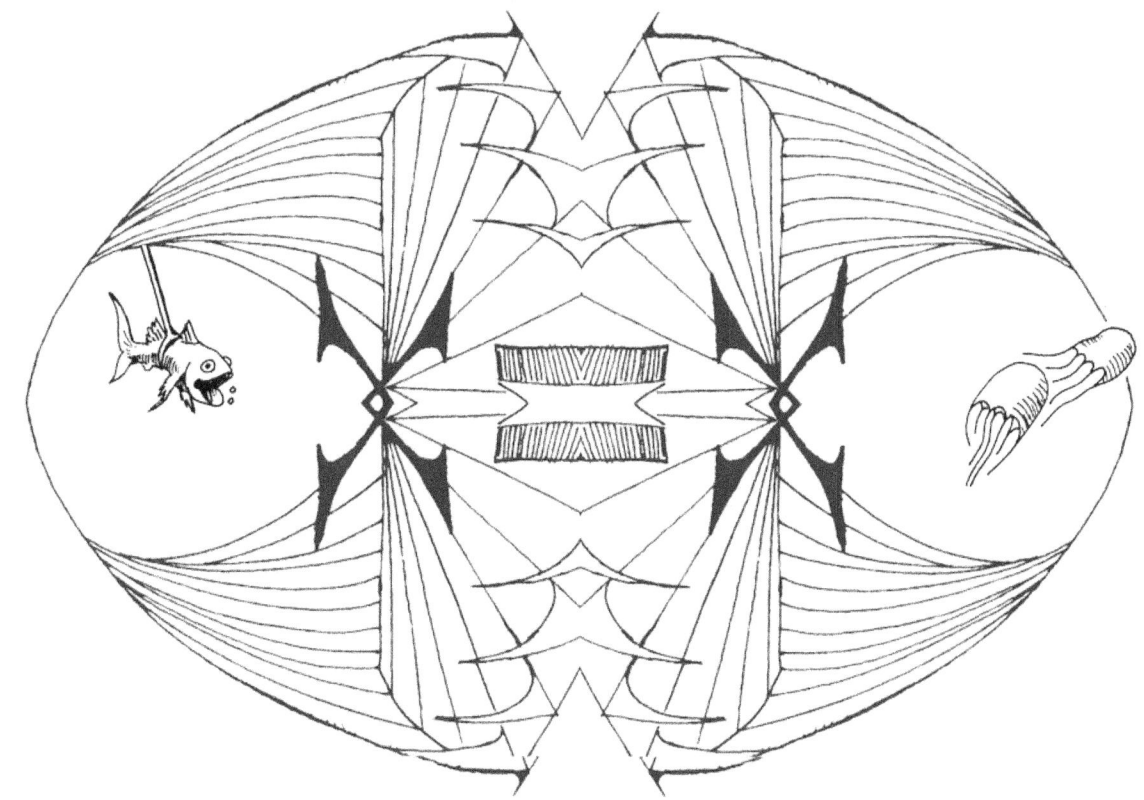

ISBN-13: 978-1548403621

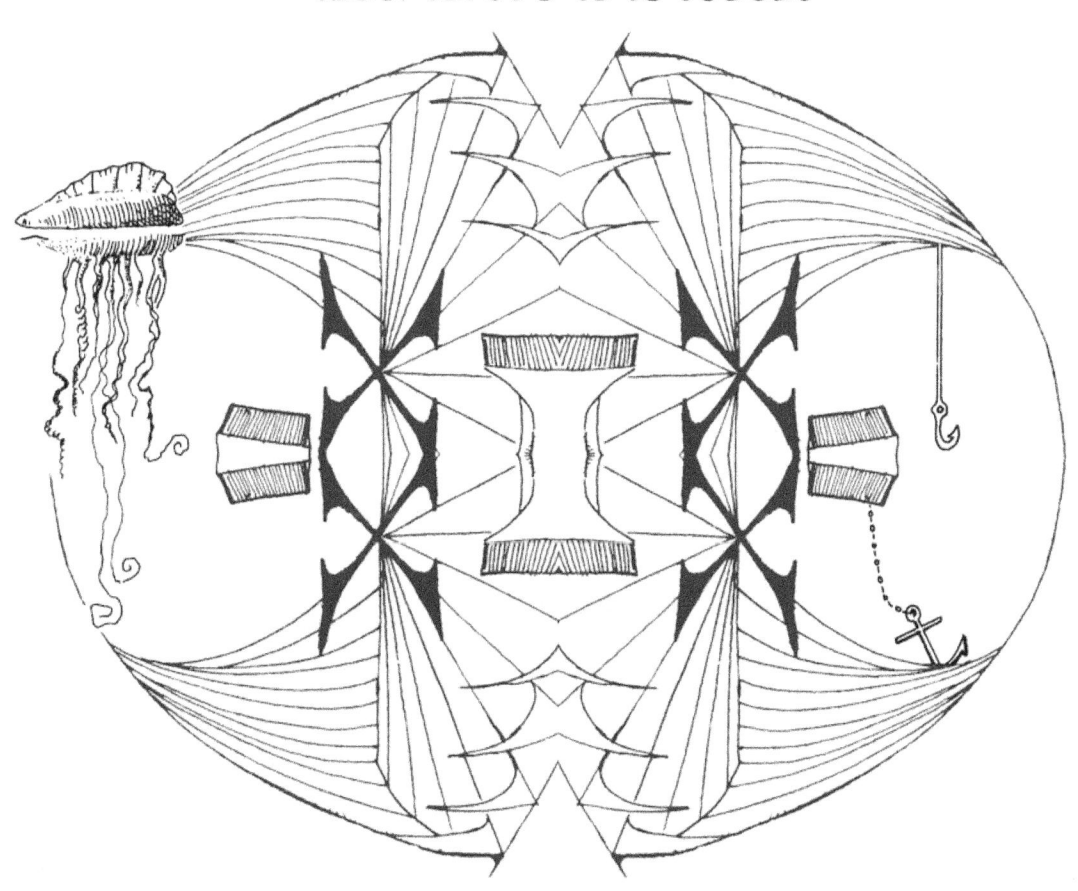

Table of Contents

1. A Road to Nowhere (1970, 9 x 12 inches)

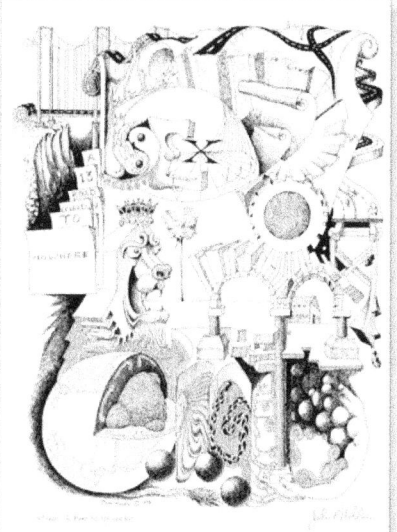

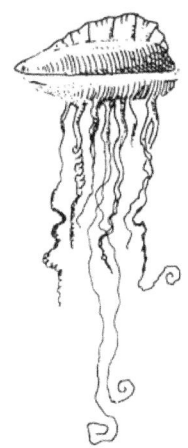

2. Crinoid Anatomy (1972, 14 x 9 inches)

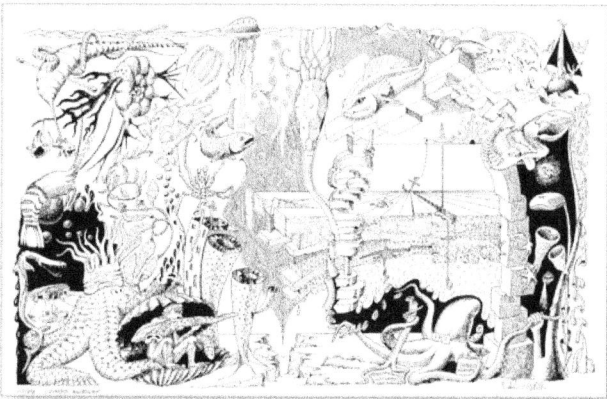

This is the order in which the prints appear in this book. Each one is immediately followed by eleven patterns made from that print. The date the print was originally created is given here in parentheses, along with the approximate size of the original.

3. Eyeball (1972, 10 x 15 inches)

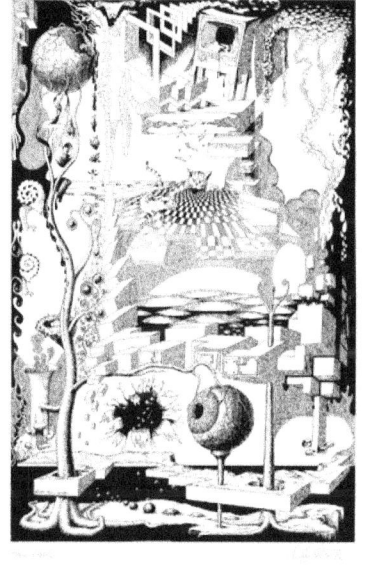

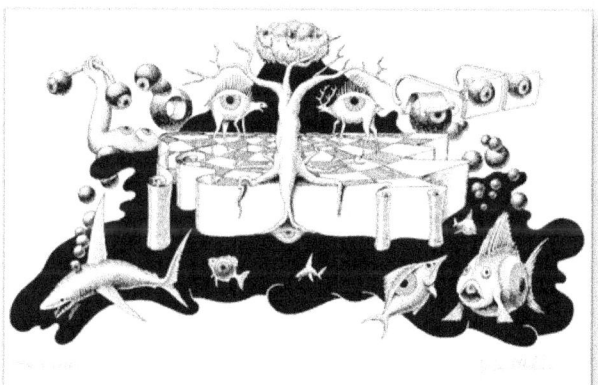

4. Eyedeas (1973, 12 x 7 inches)

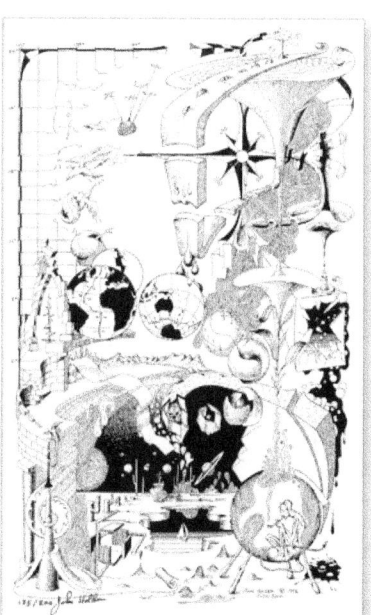

5. Cubic Earth (1972, 9 x 19 inches)

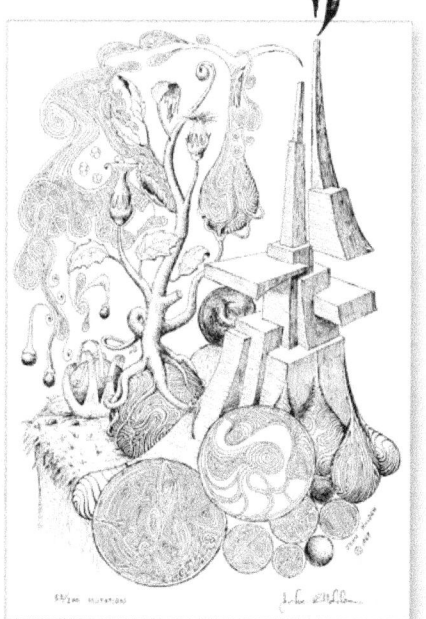

6. Mutation (1969, 8 x 11 inches)

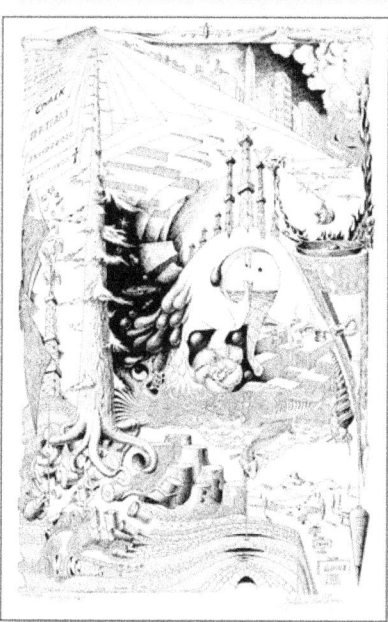

7. Geoecology (1970, 9 x 15 inches)

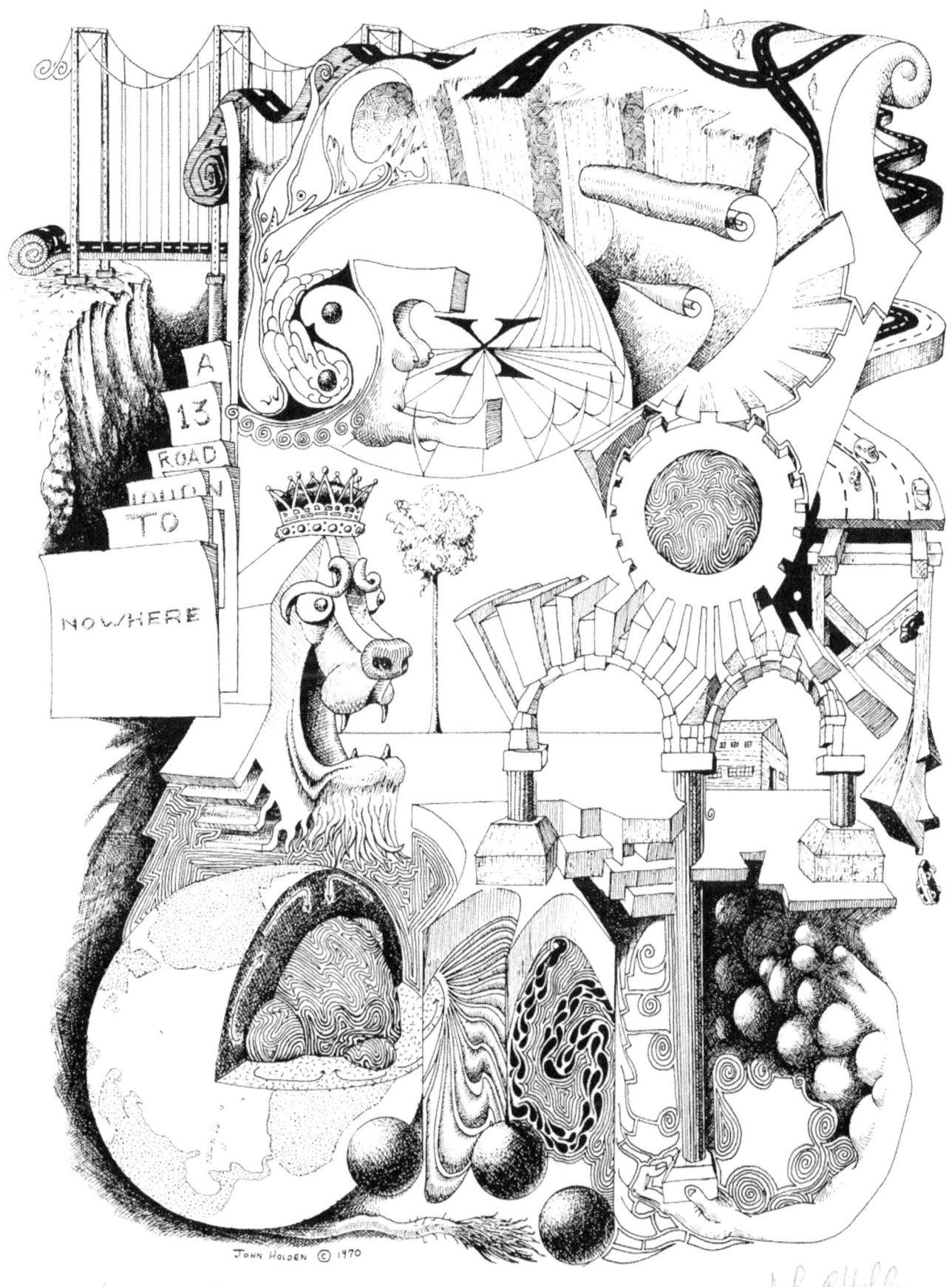

A
13
ROAD
TO
NOWHERE

NOWHERE

John Holden © 1970

John C Holden

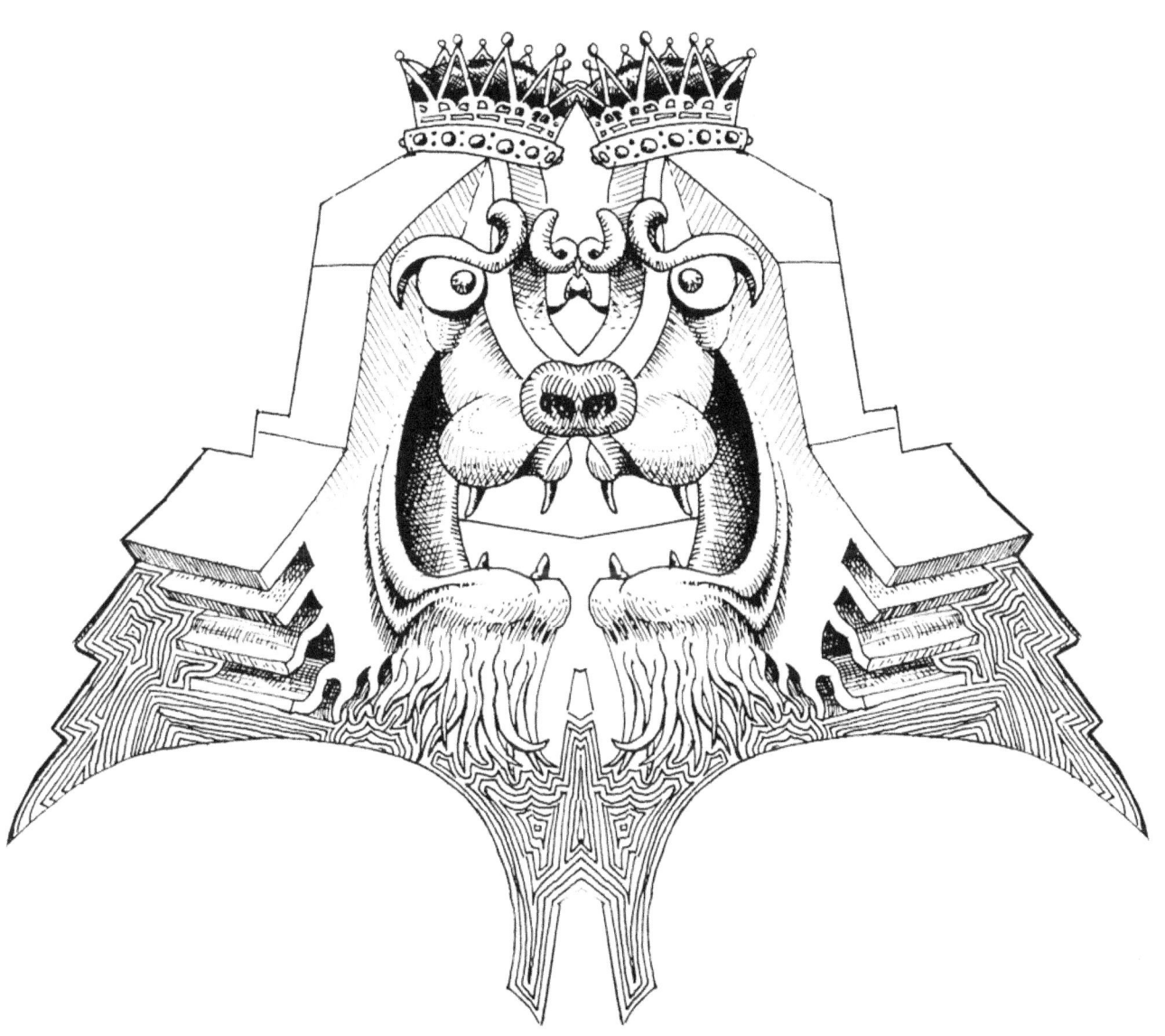

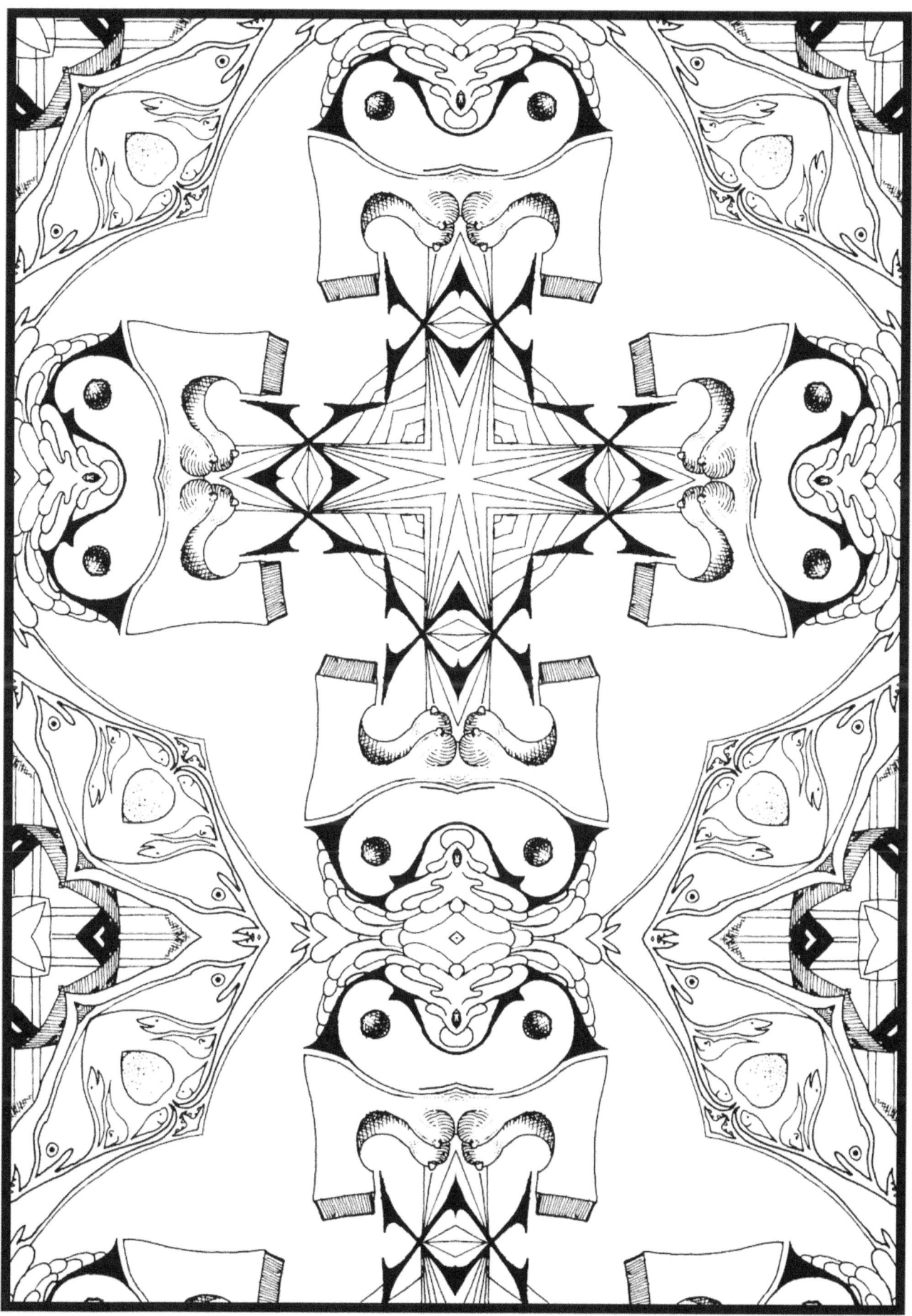

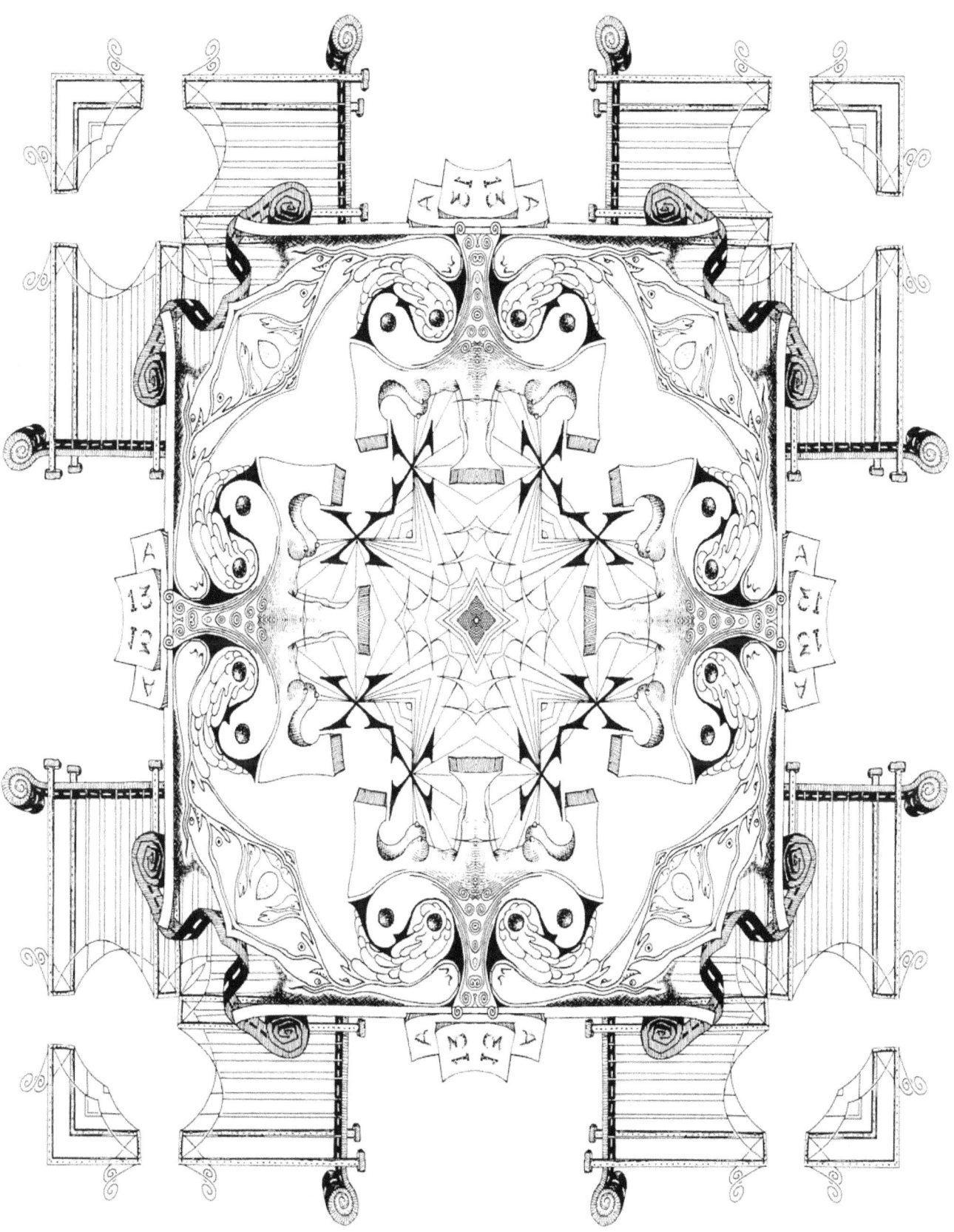

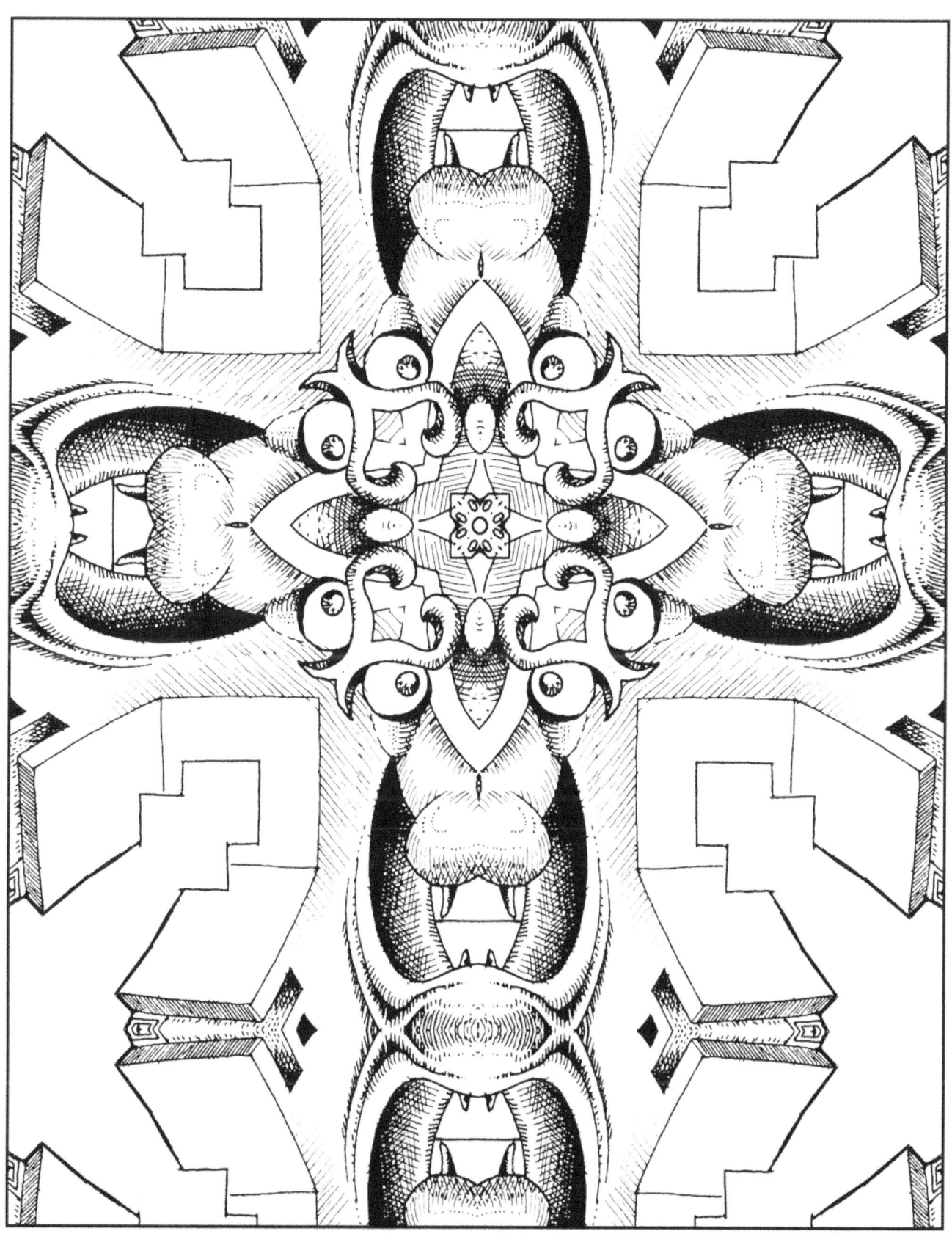

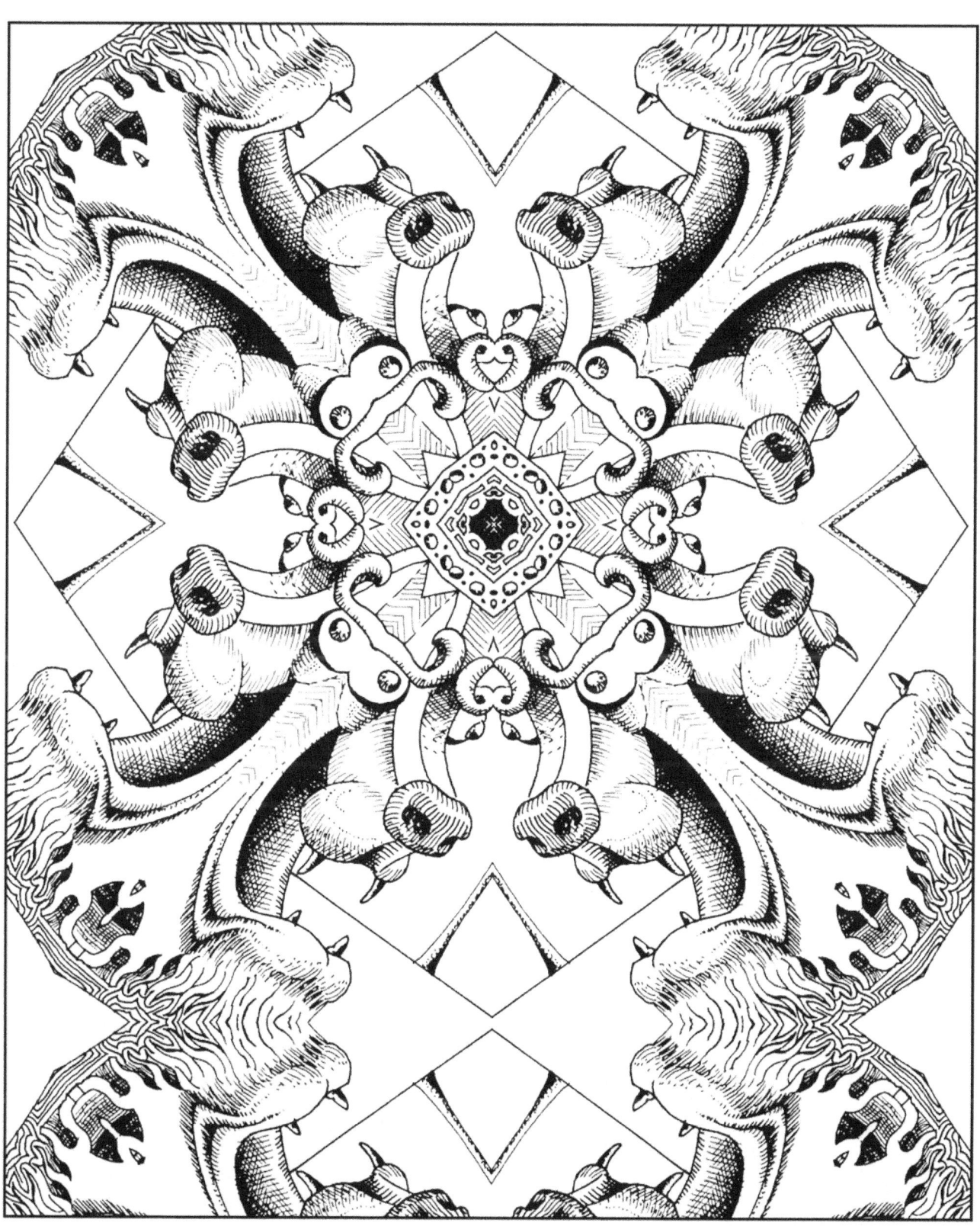

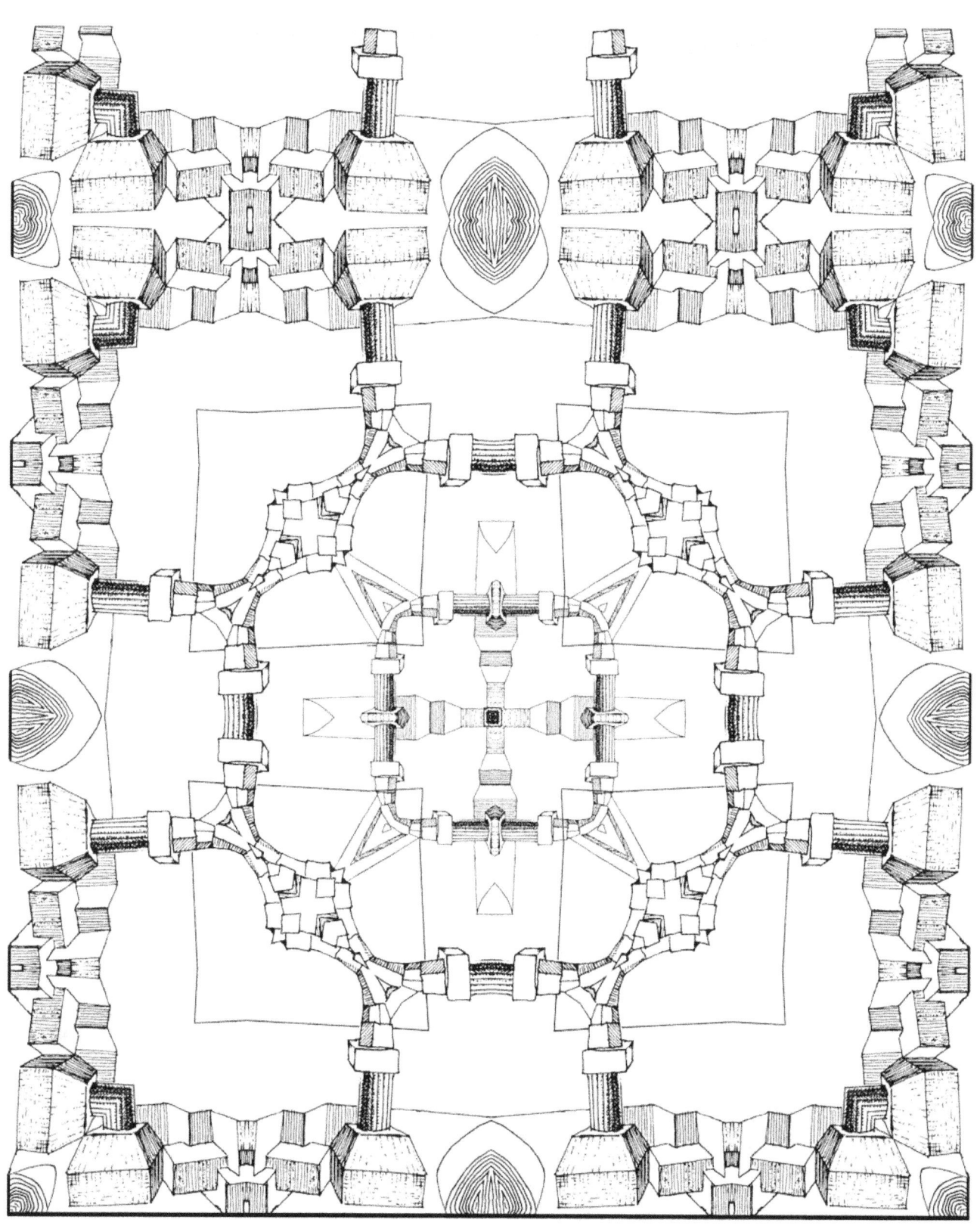

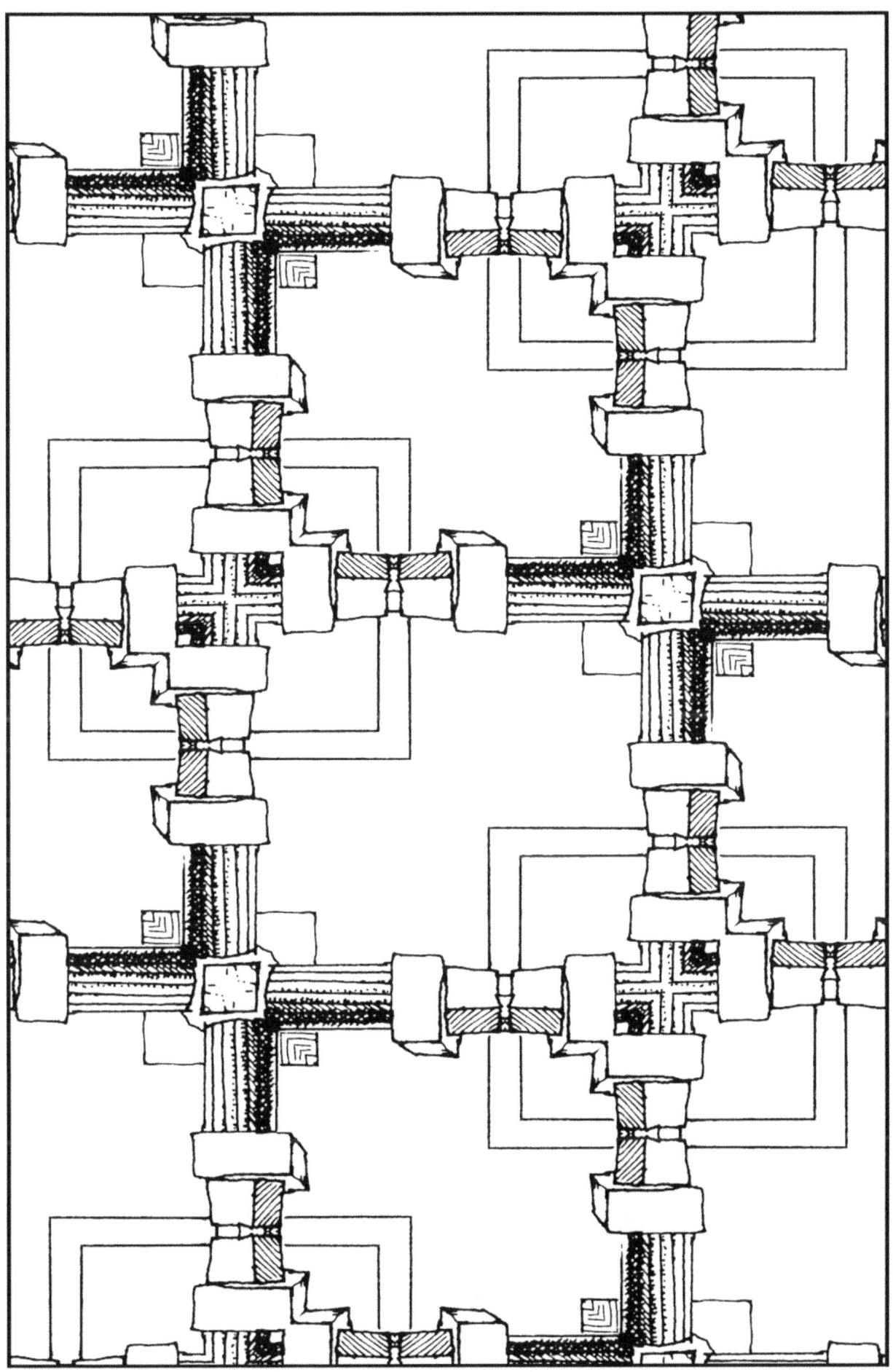

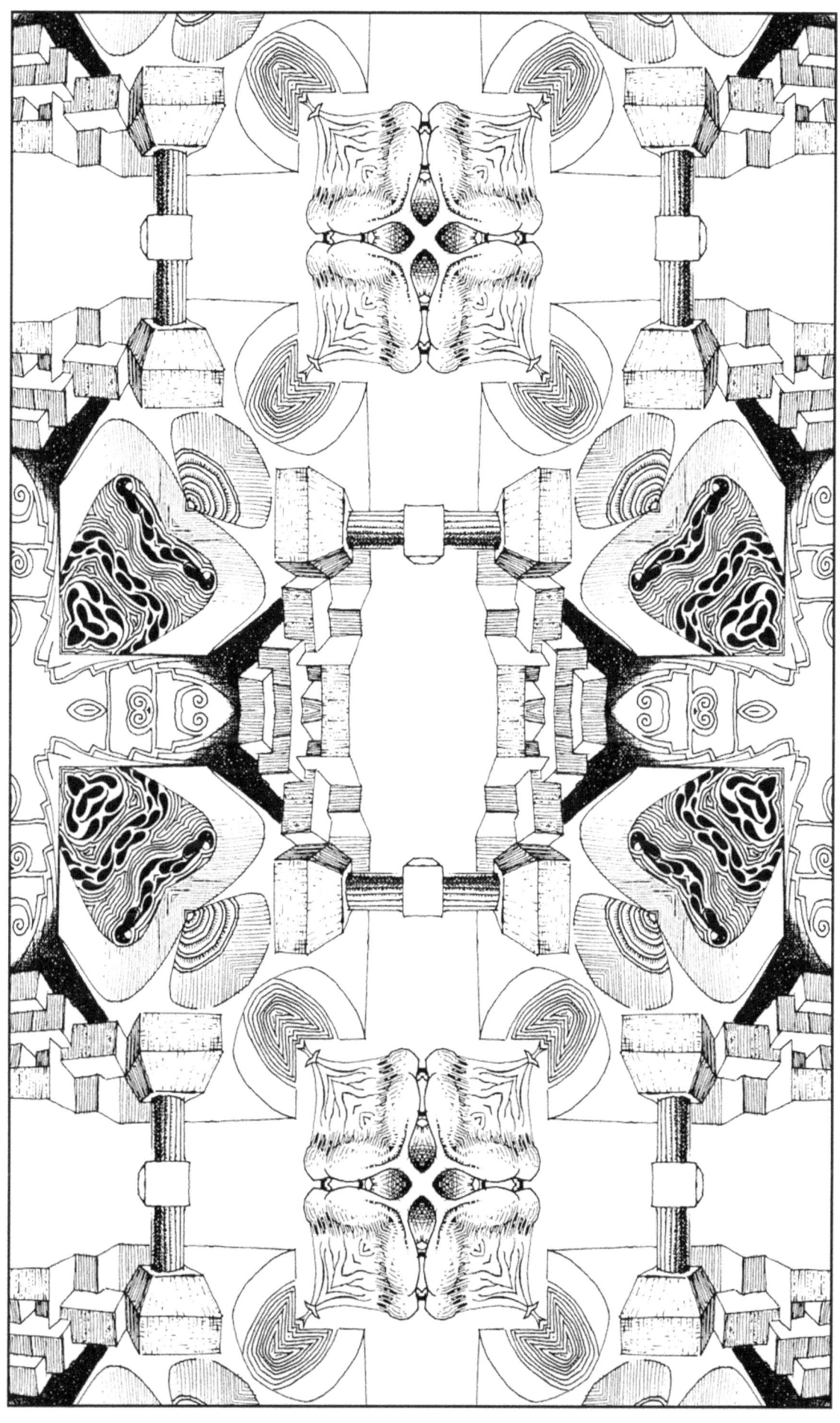

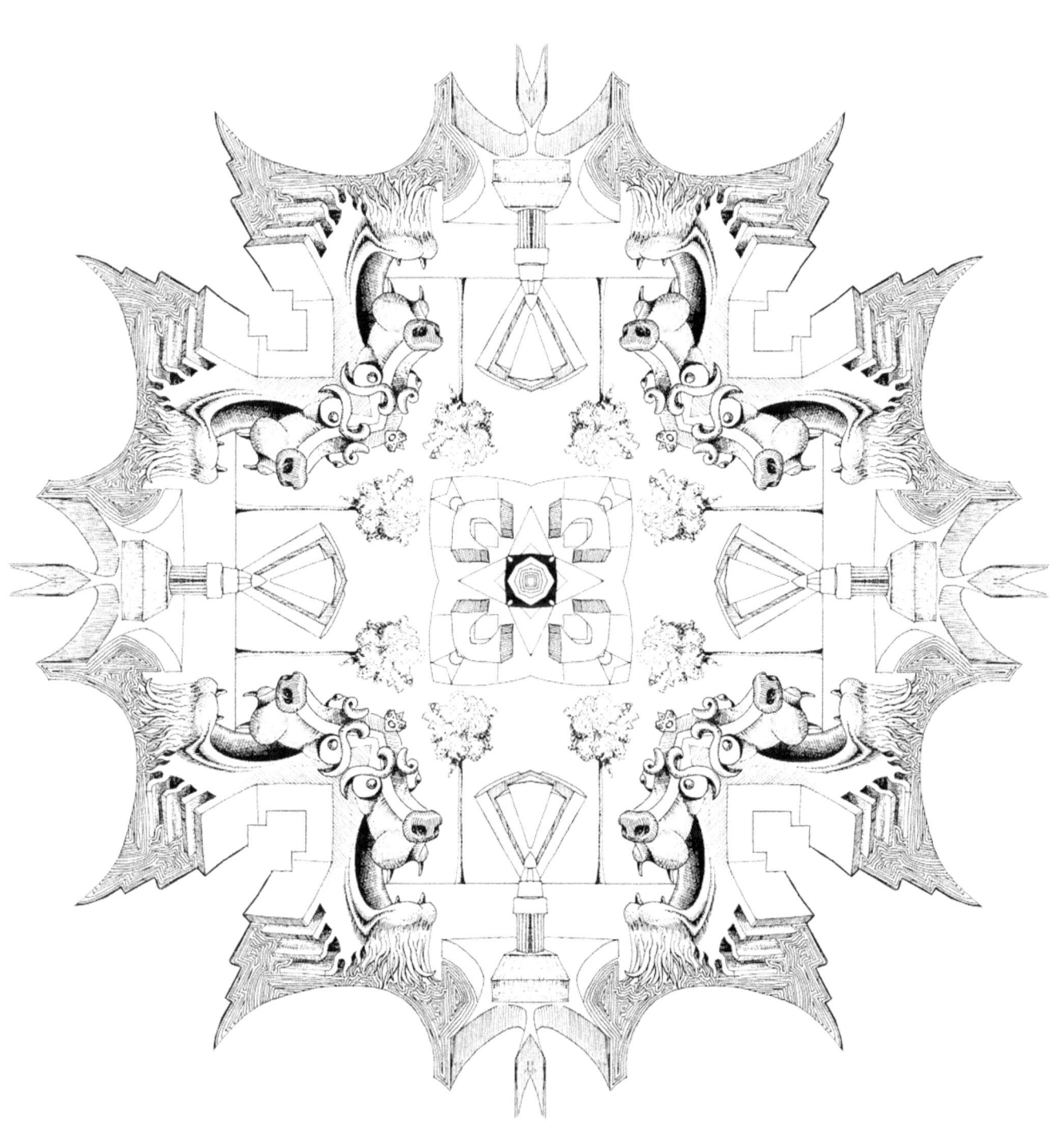

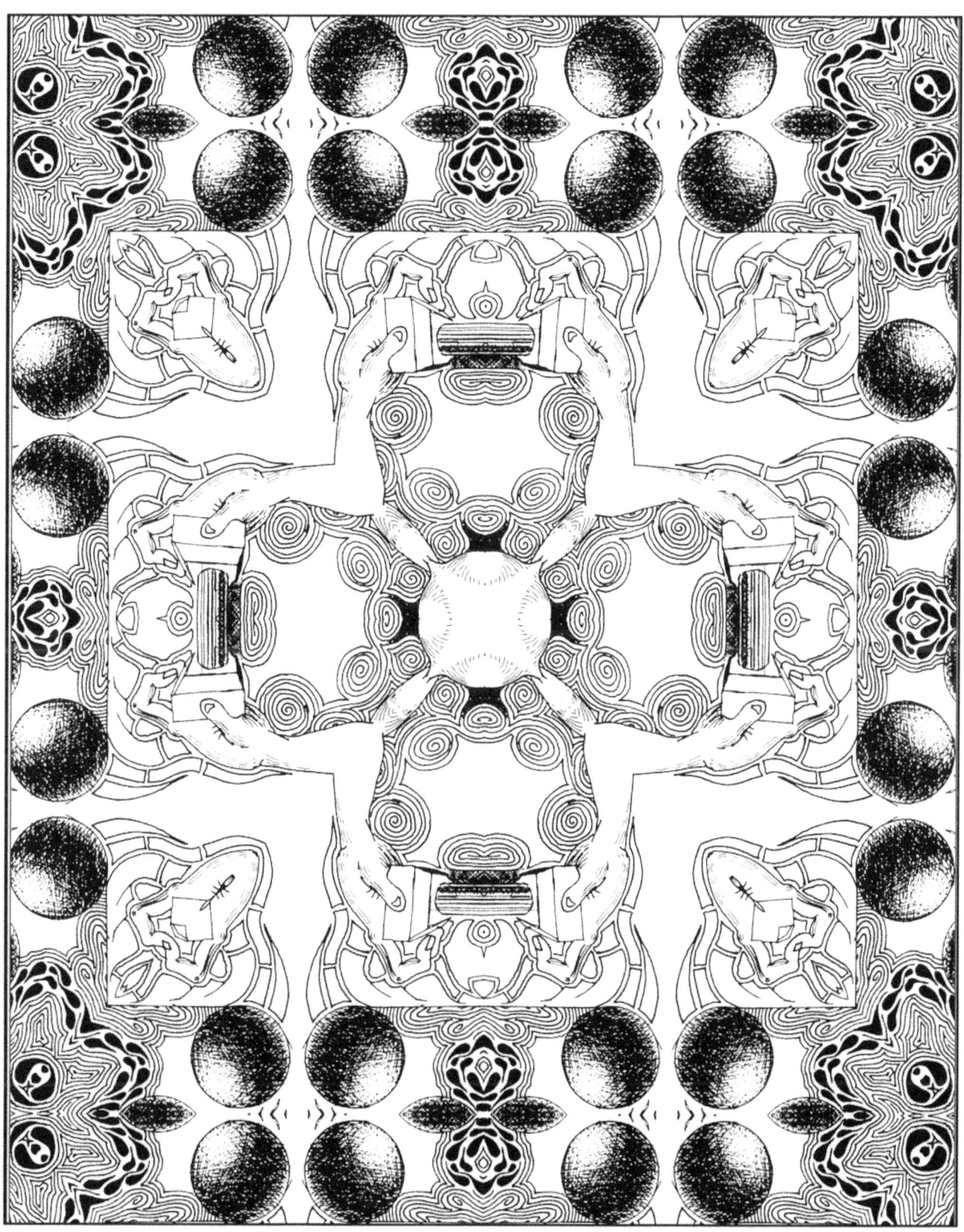

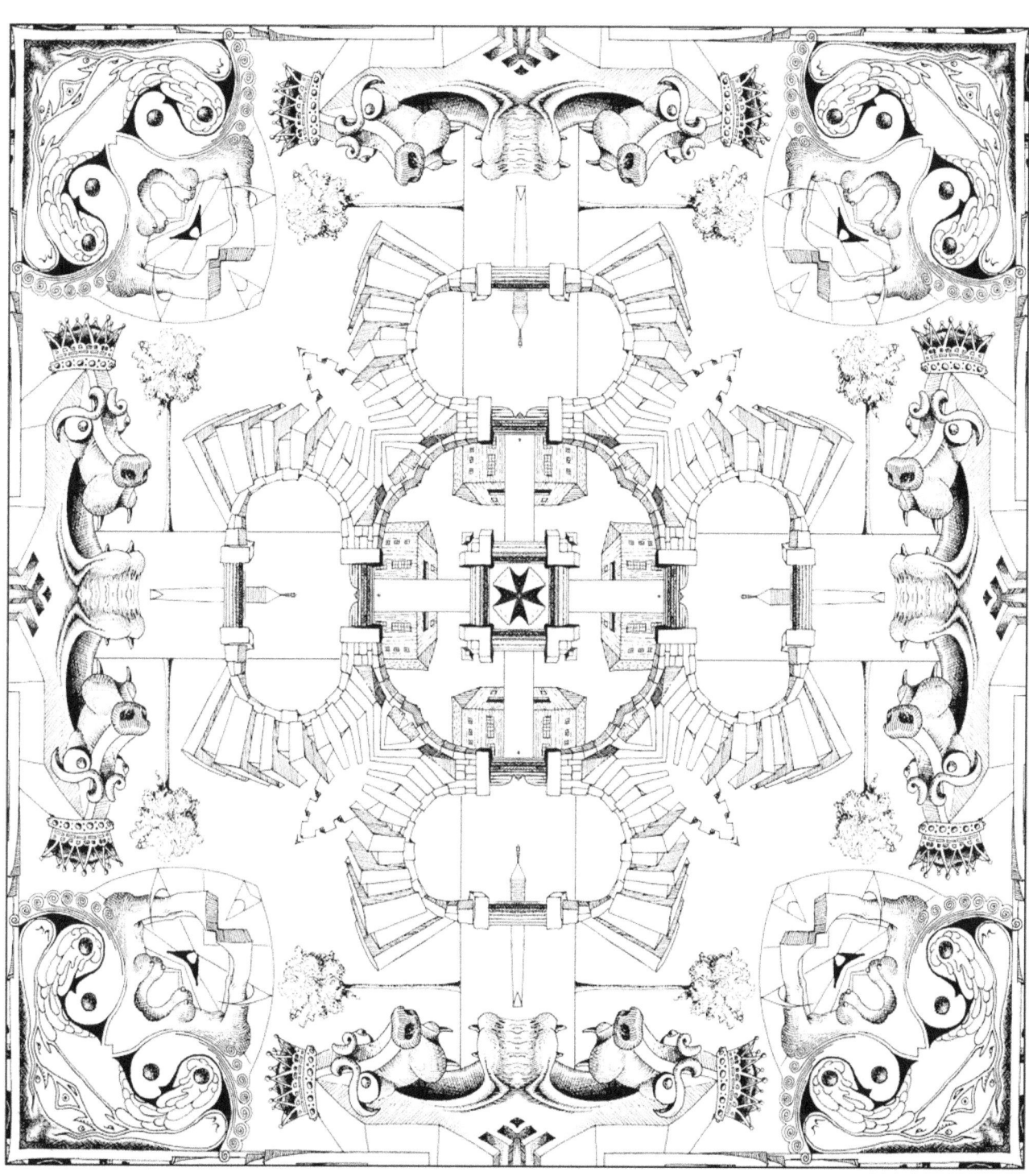

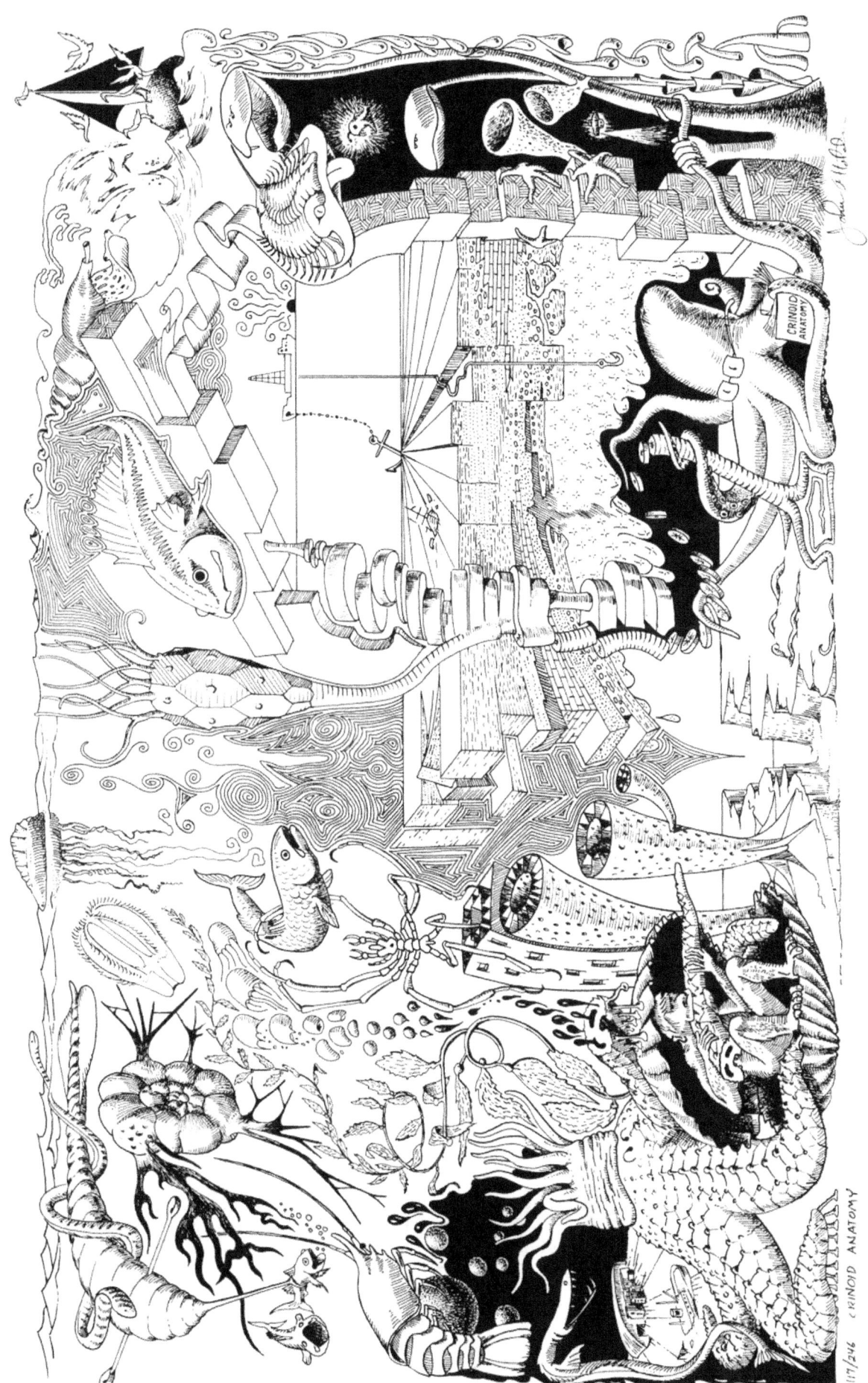

CRINOD ANATOMY

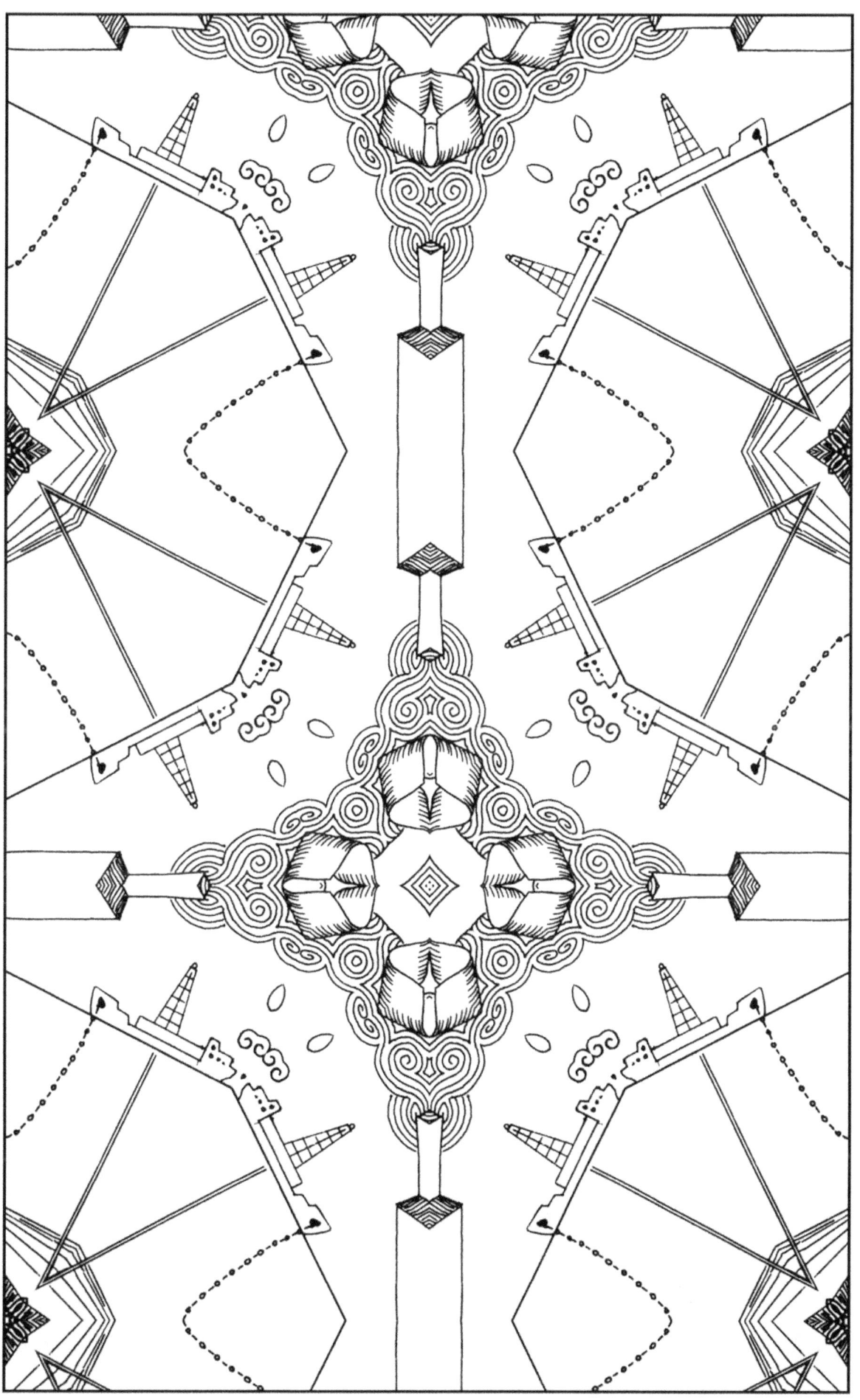

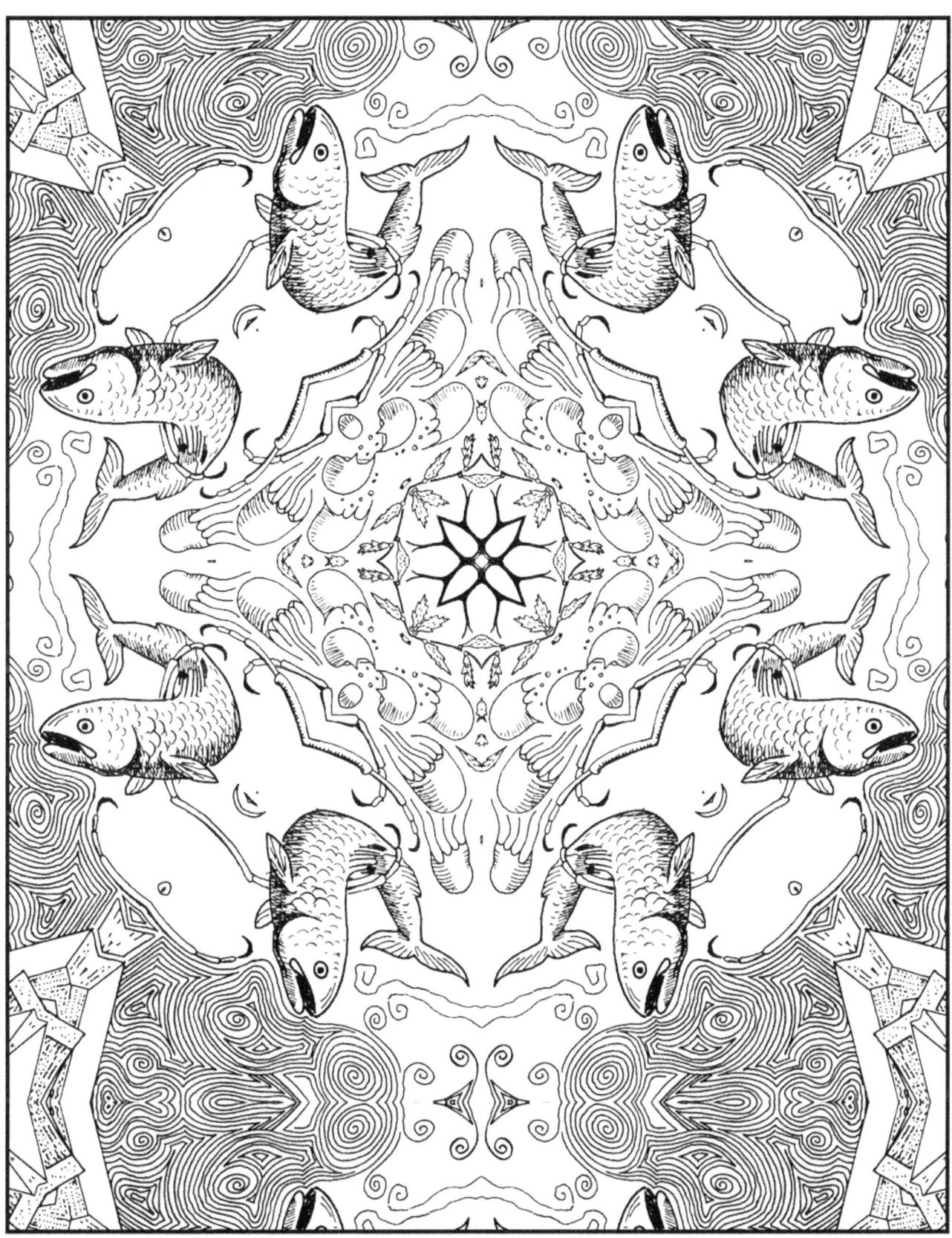

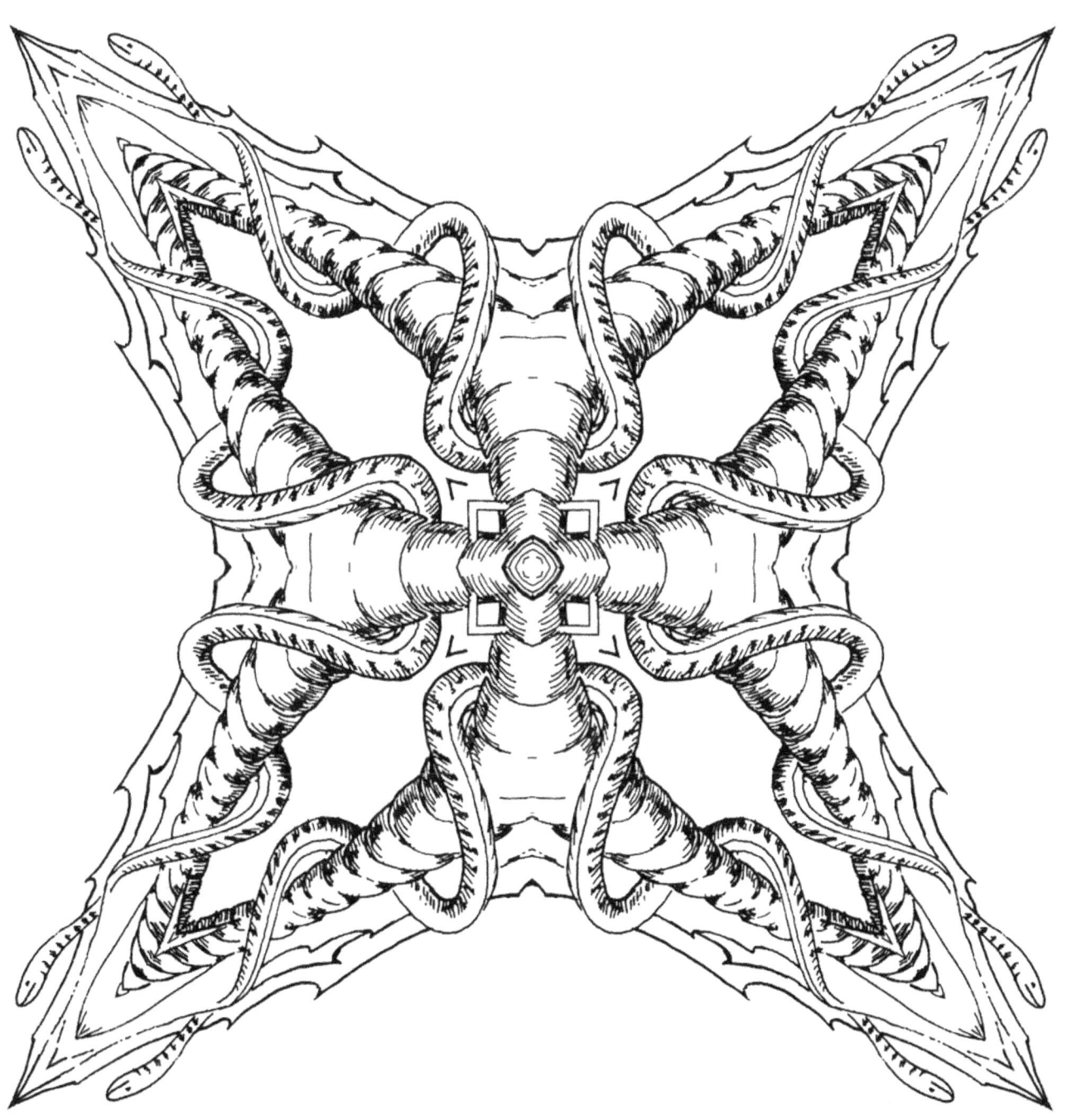

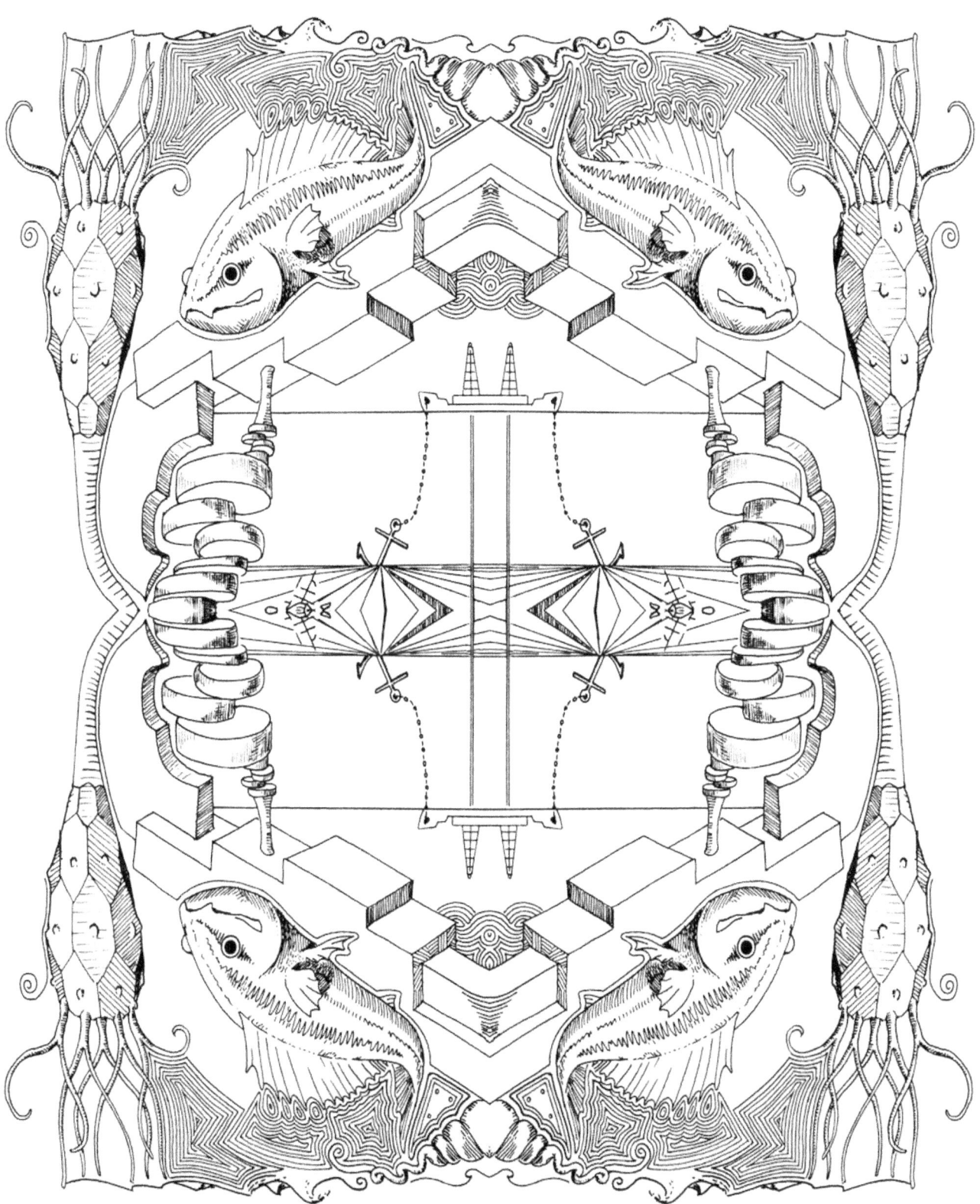

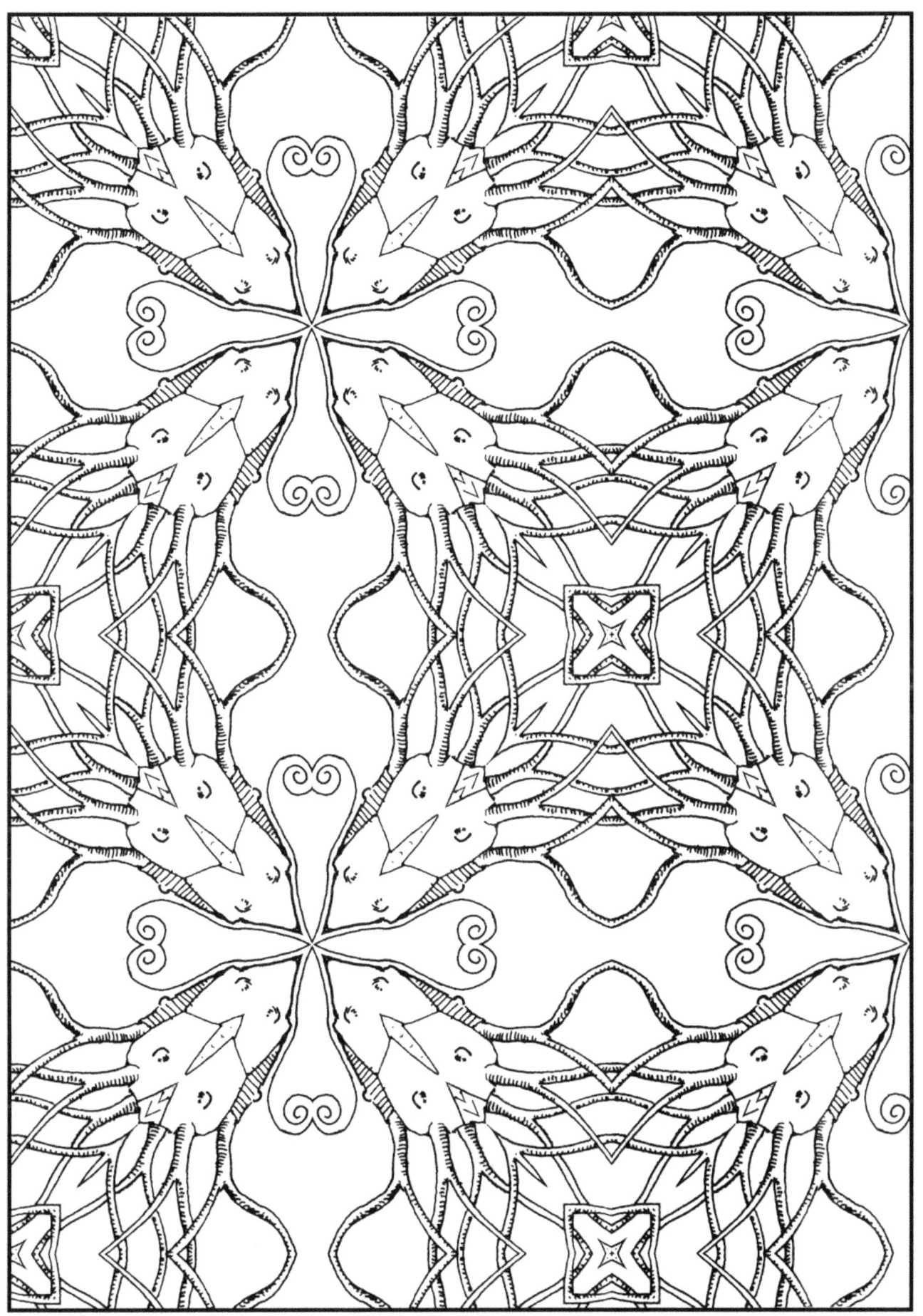

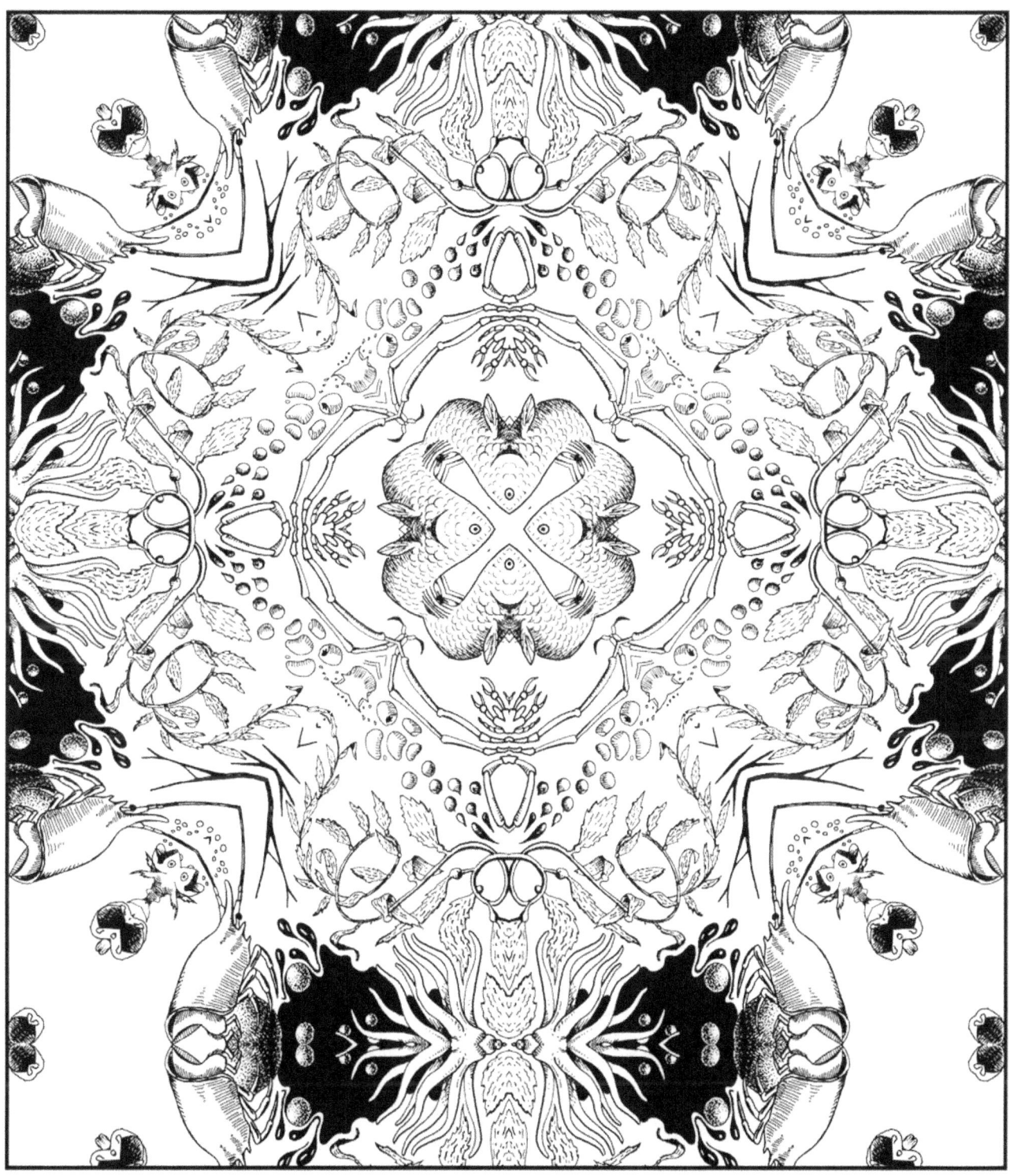

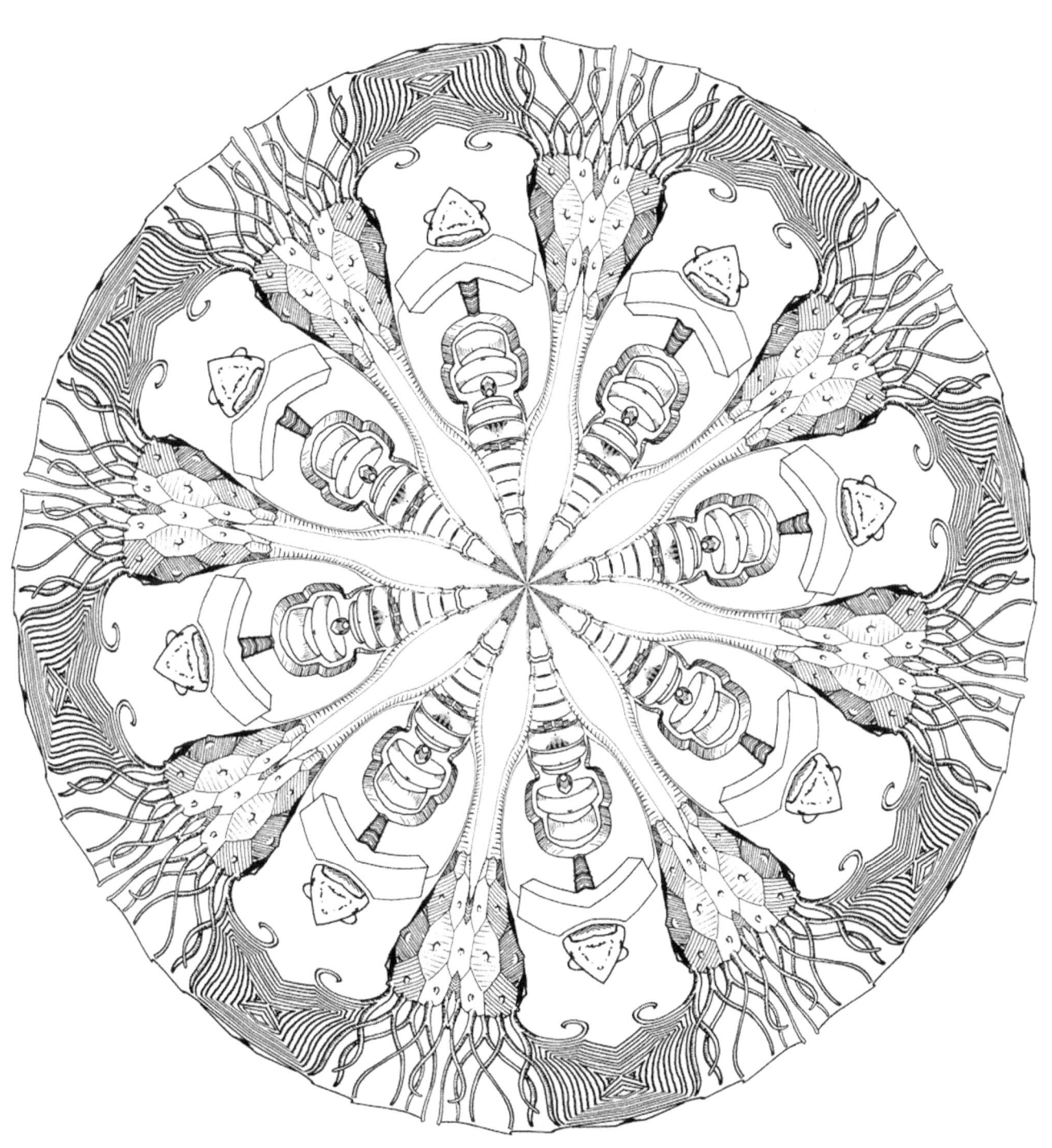

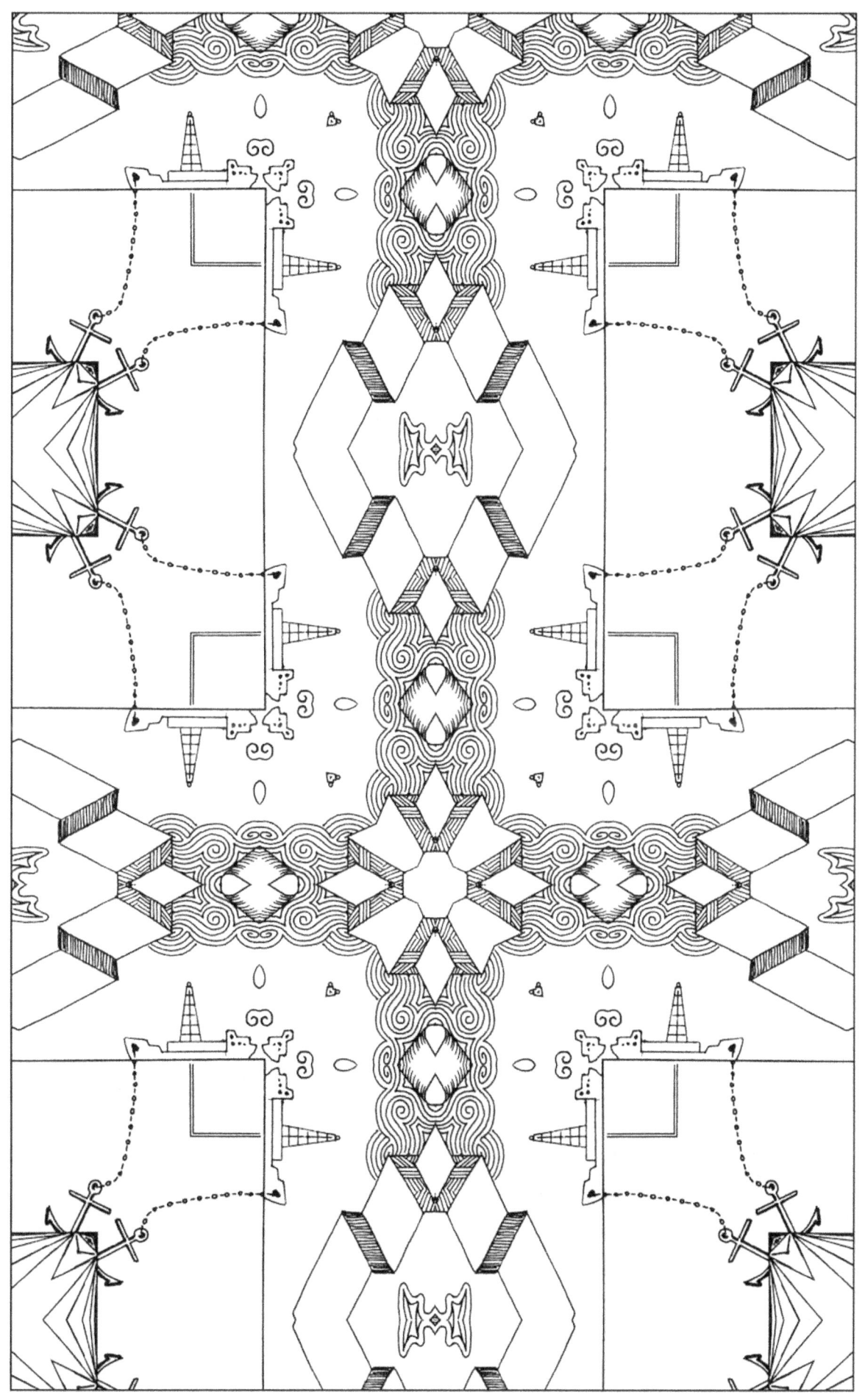

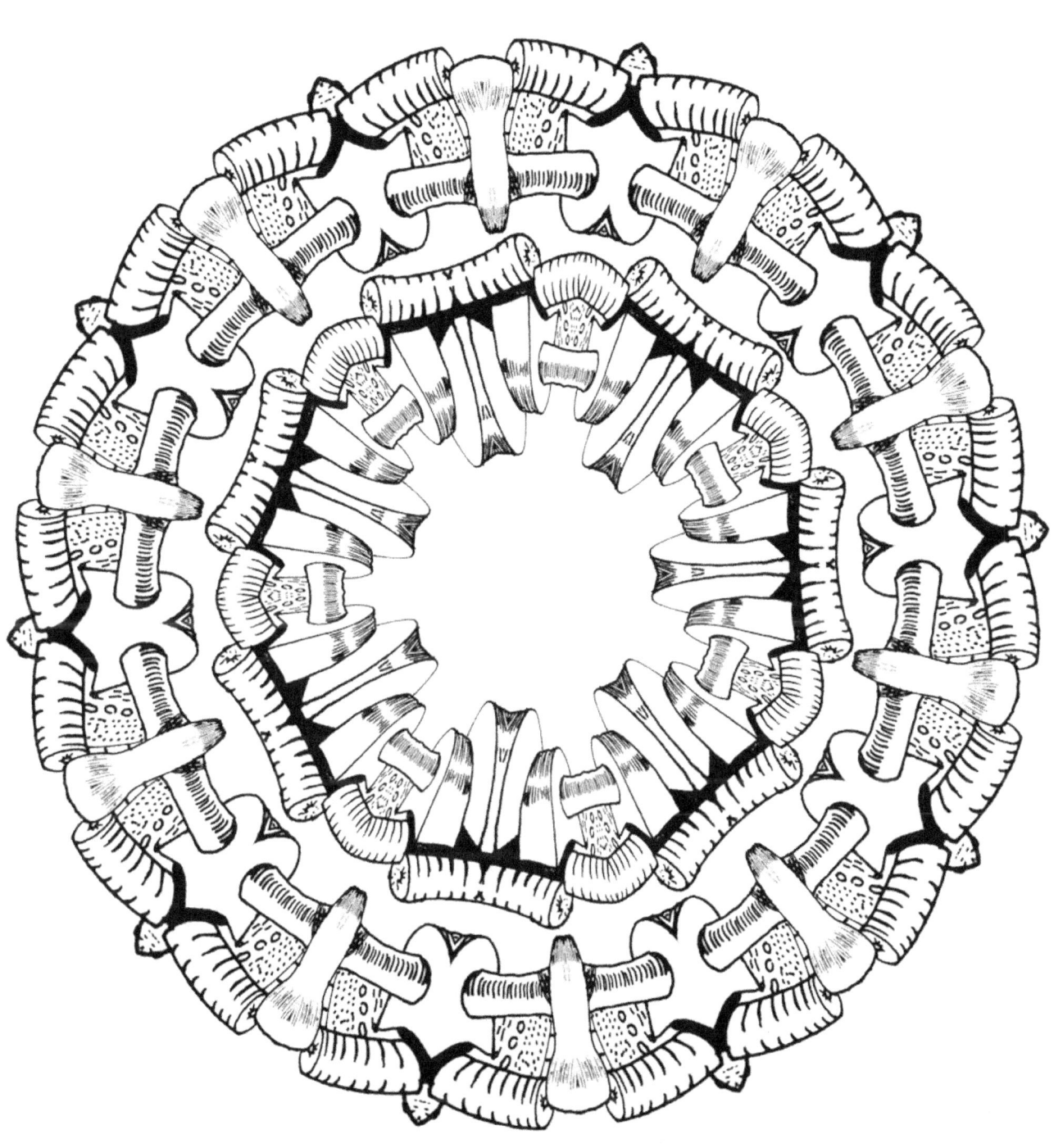

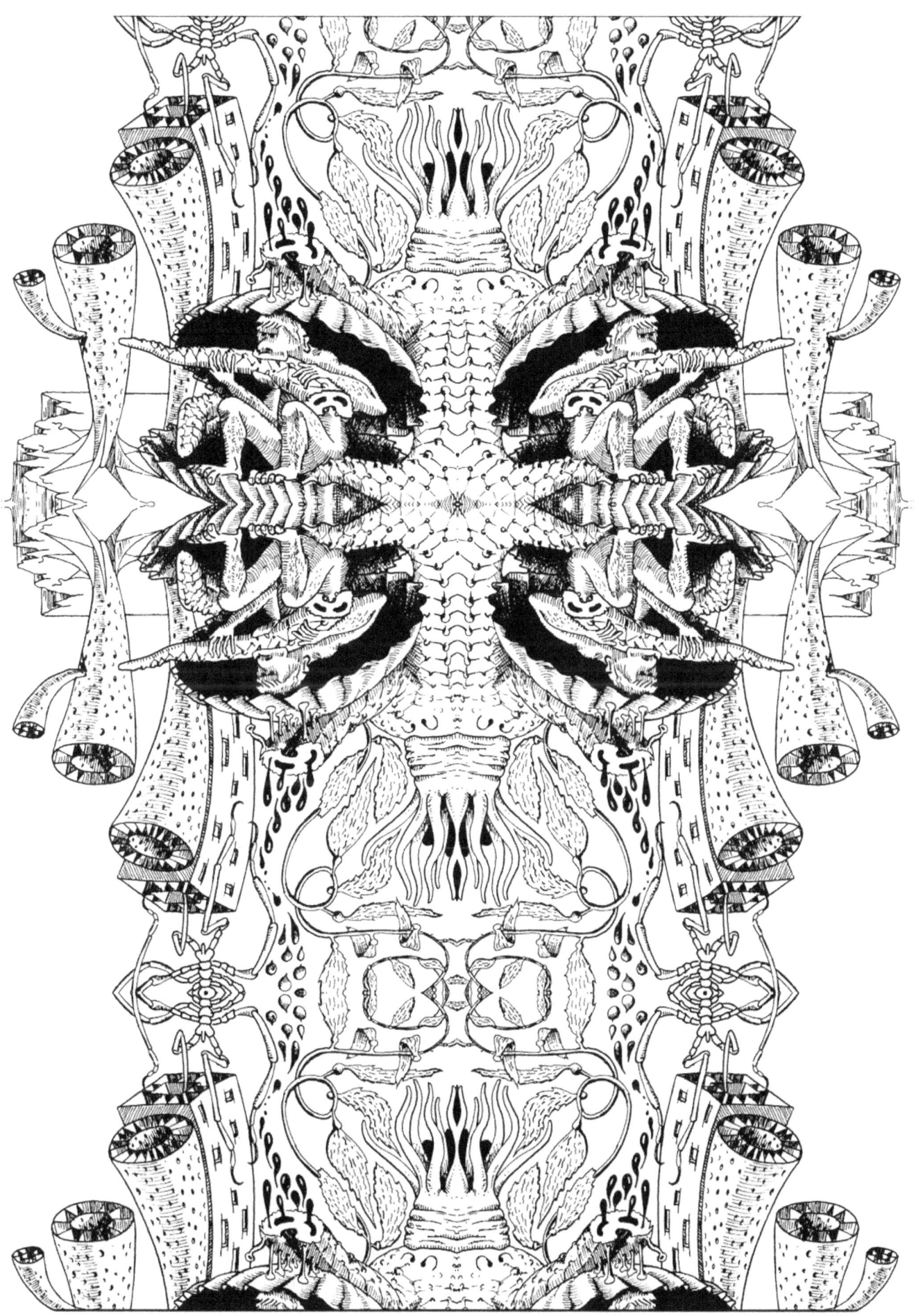

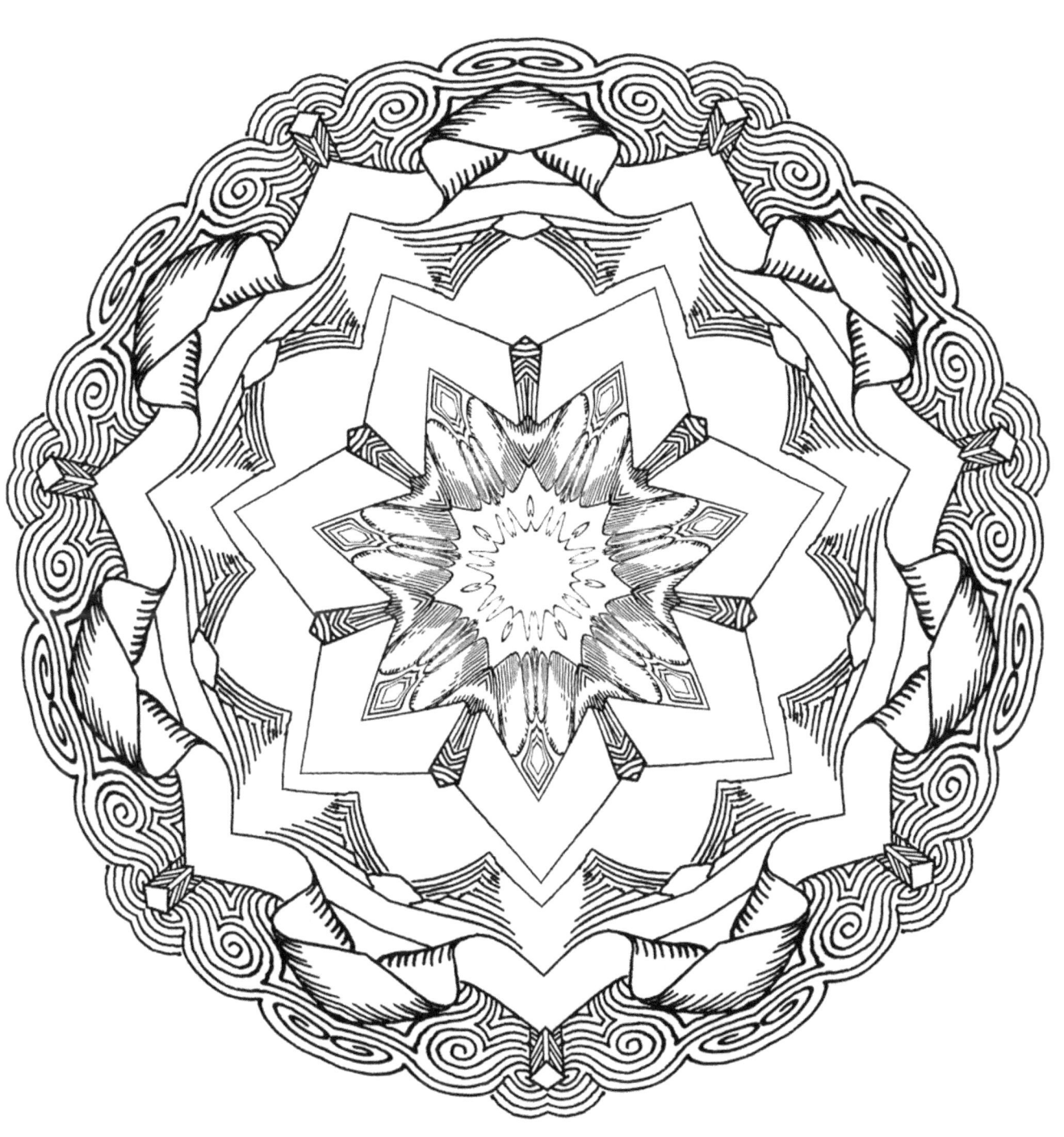

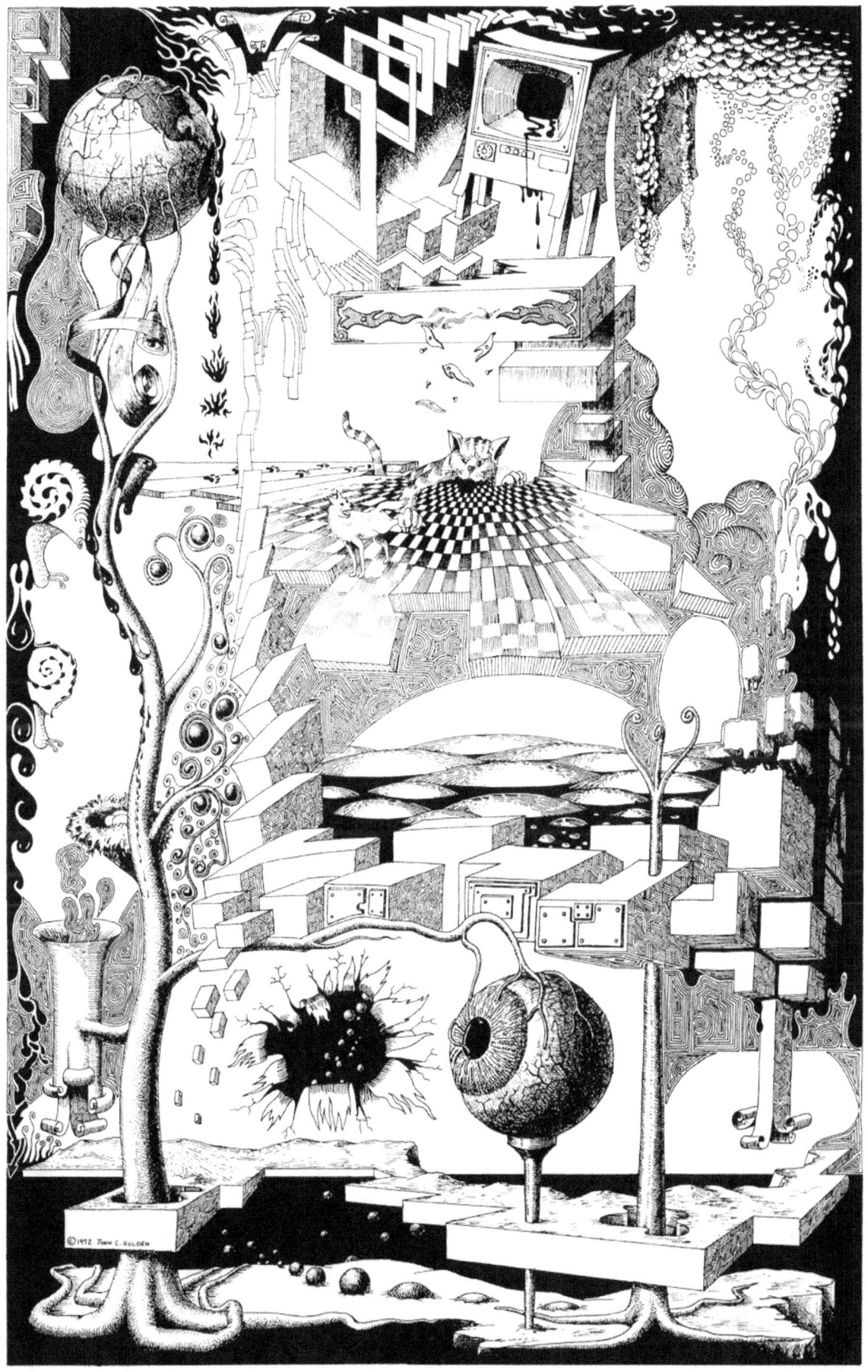

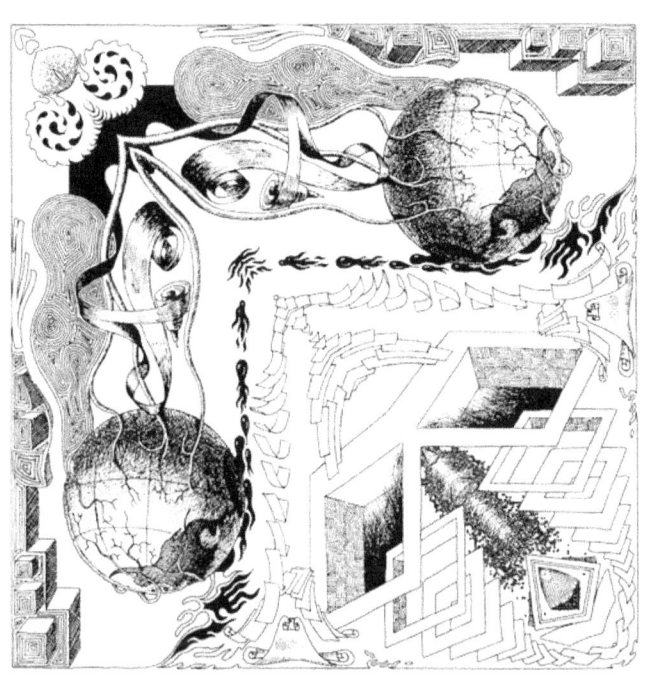
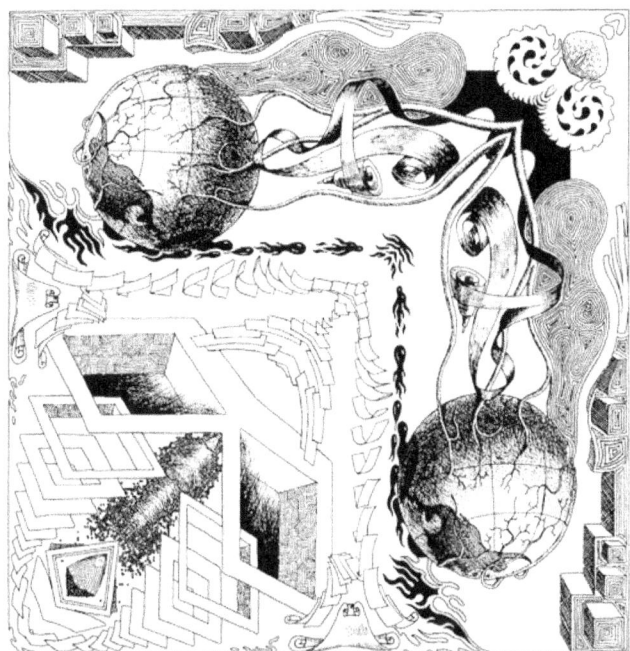
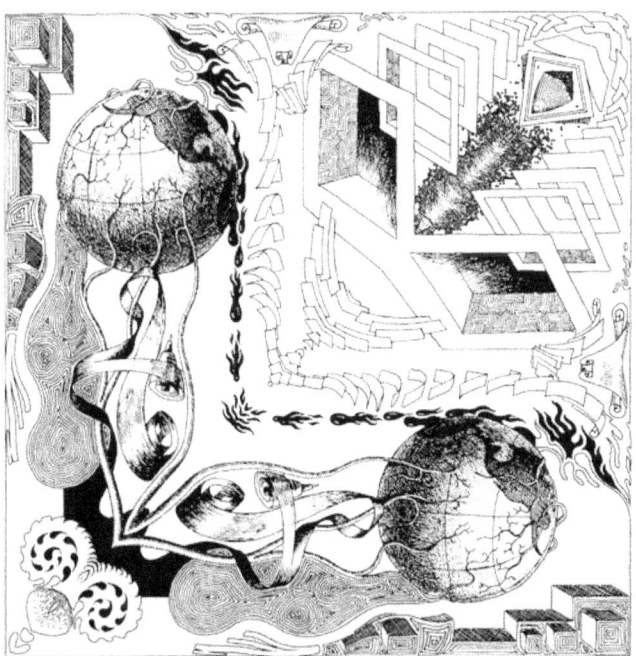
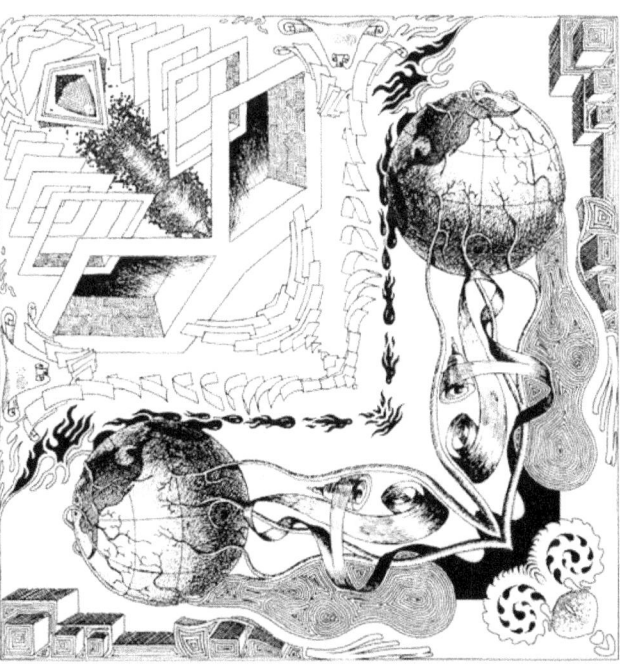

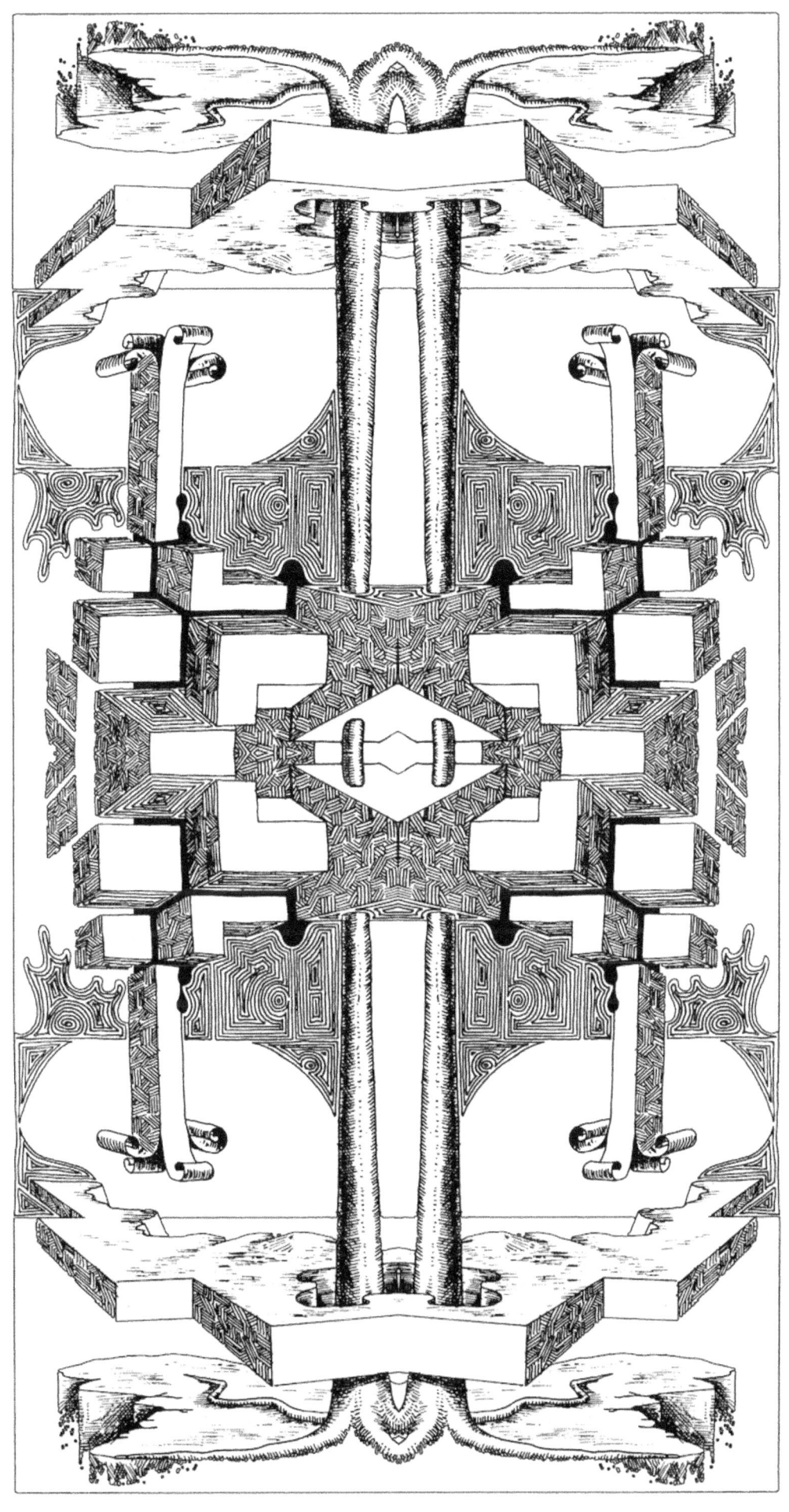

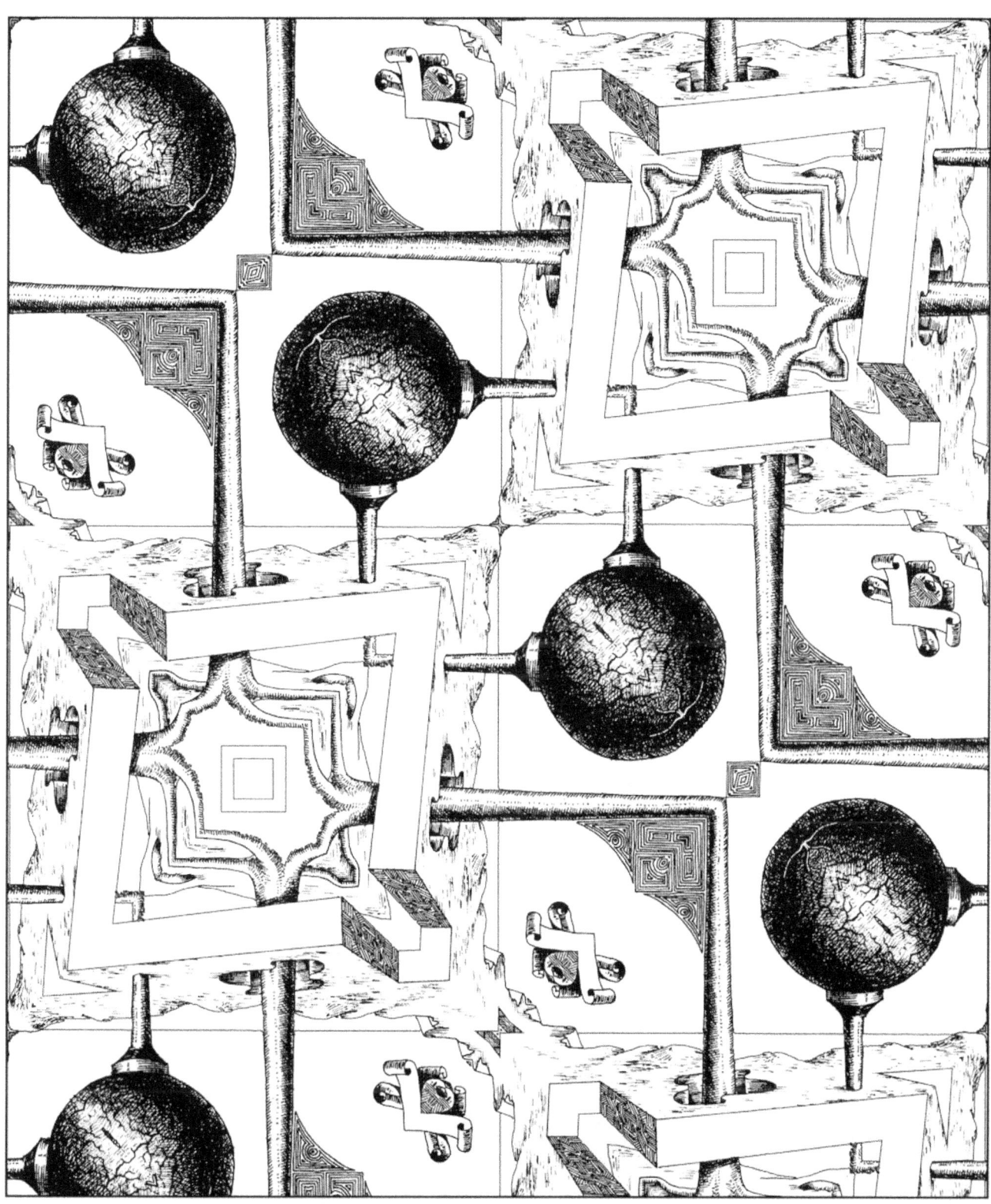

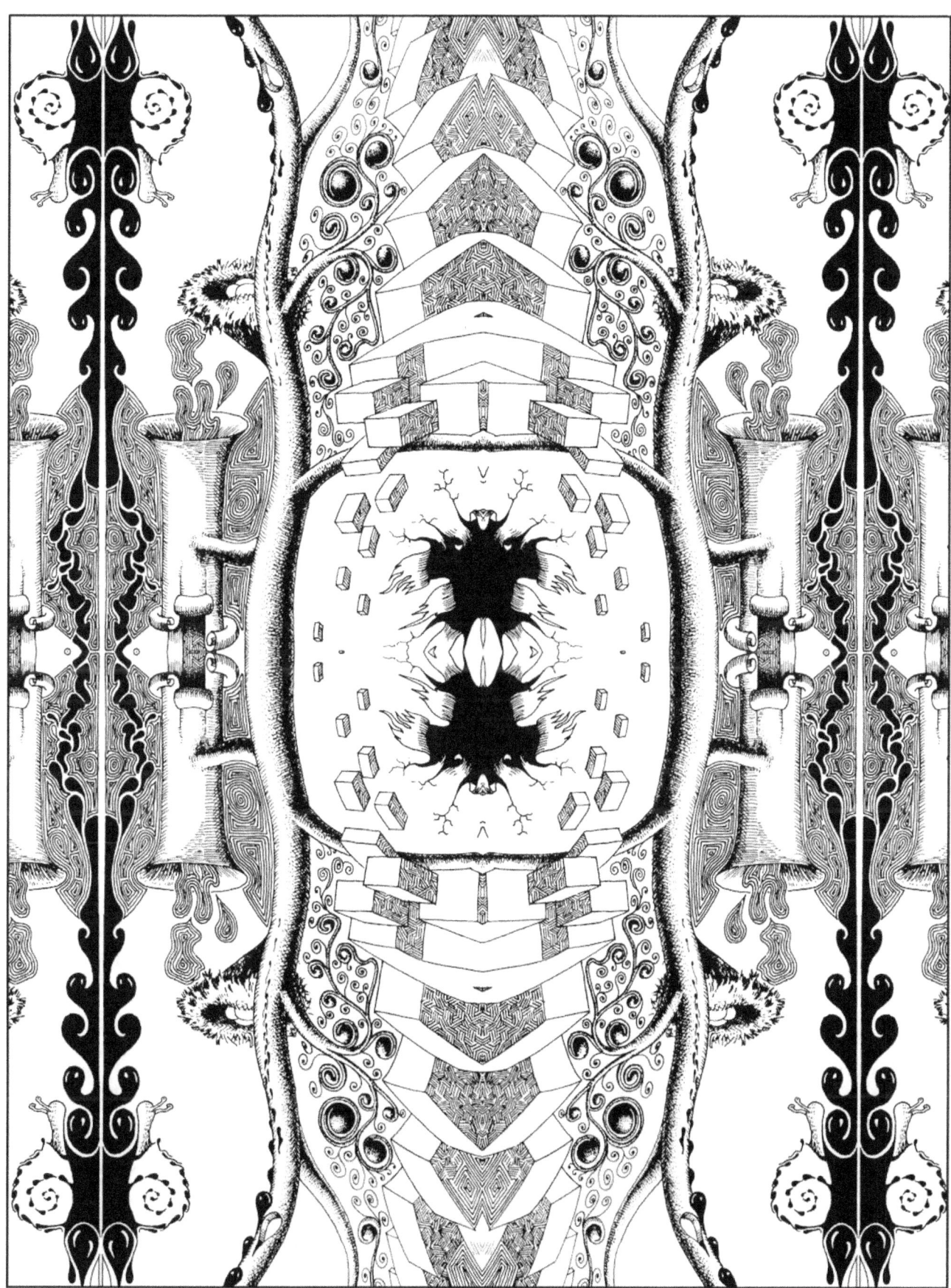

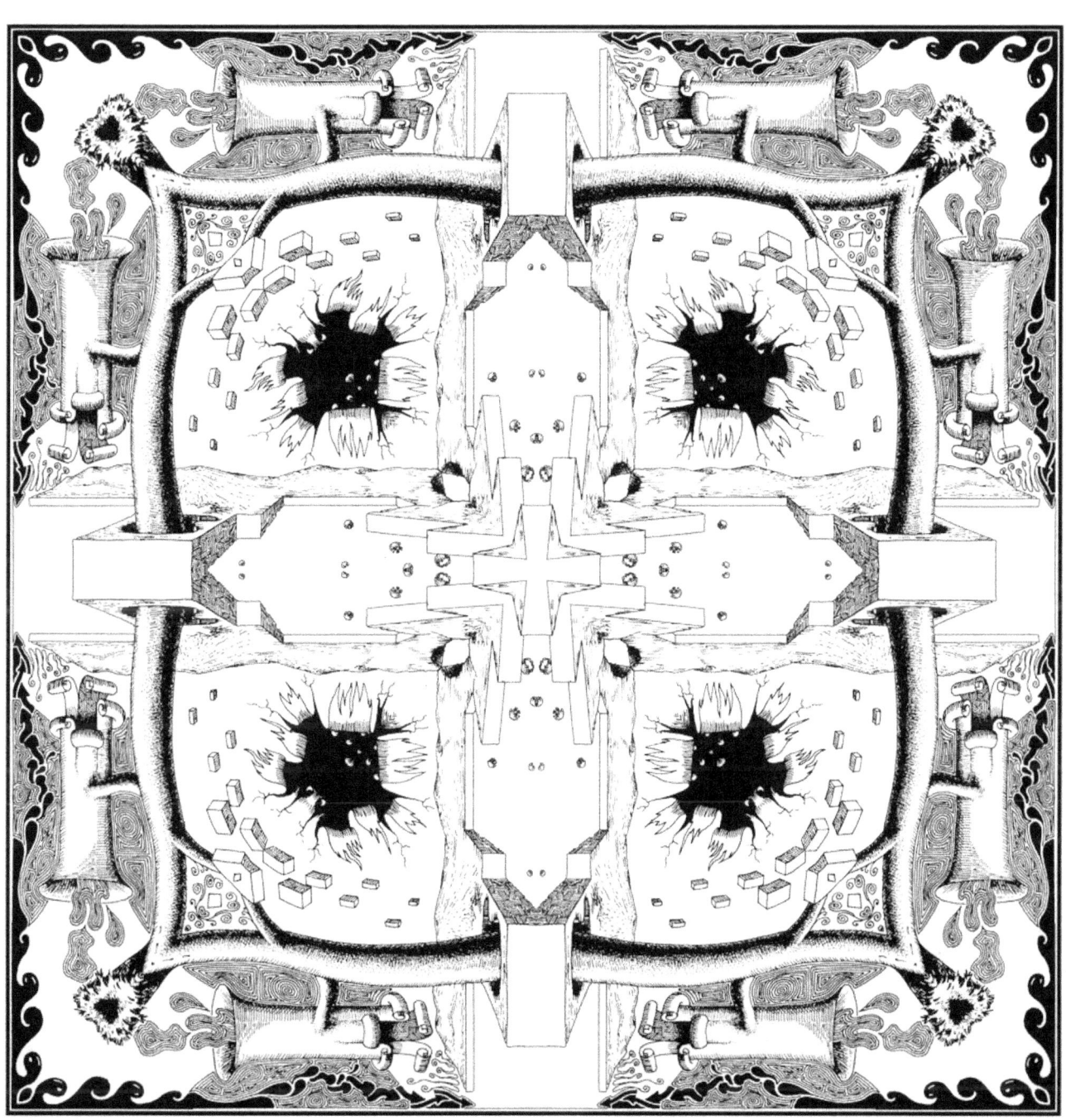

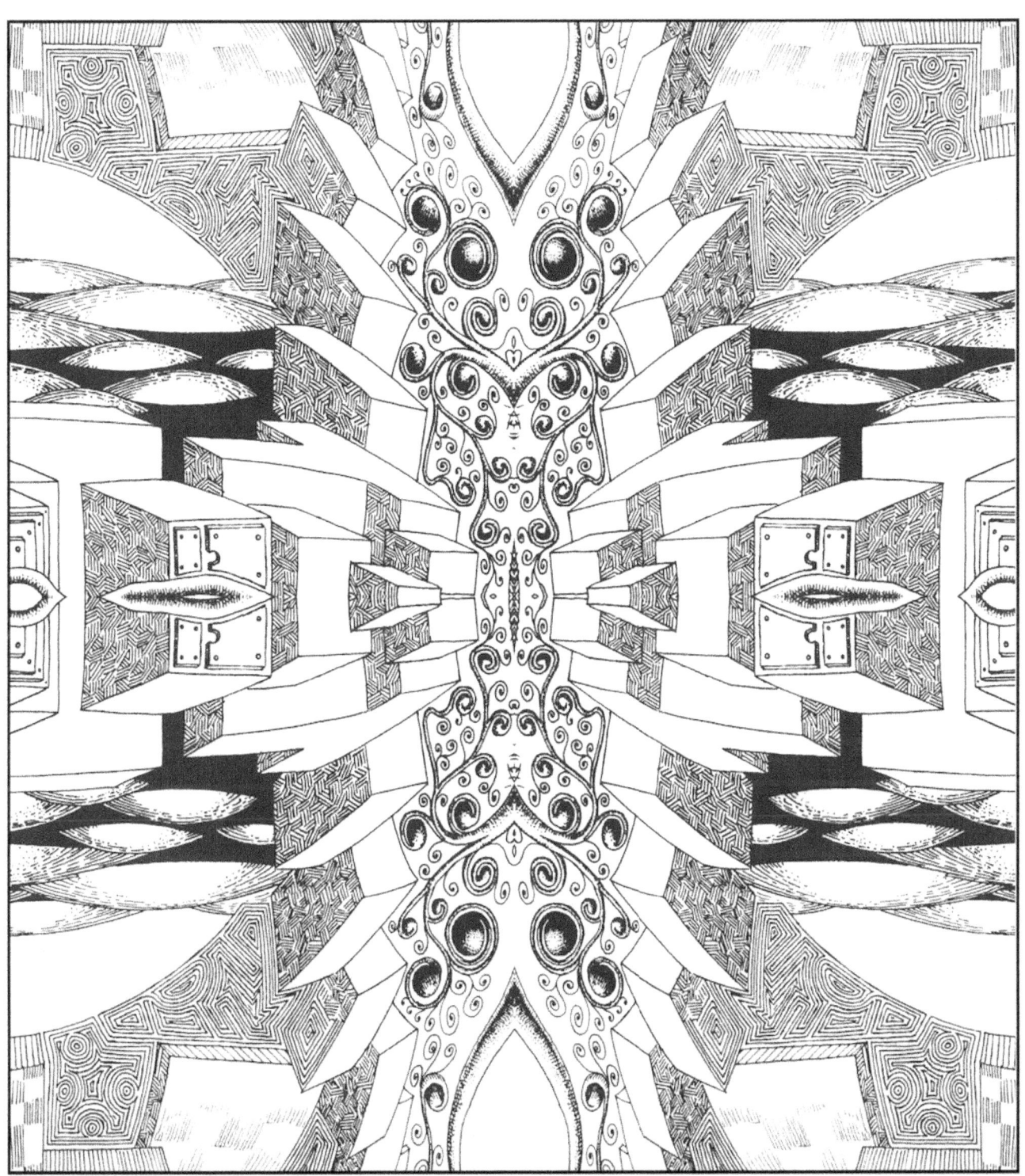

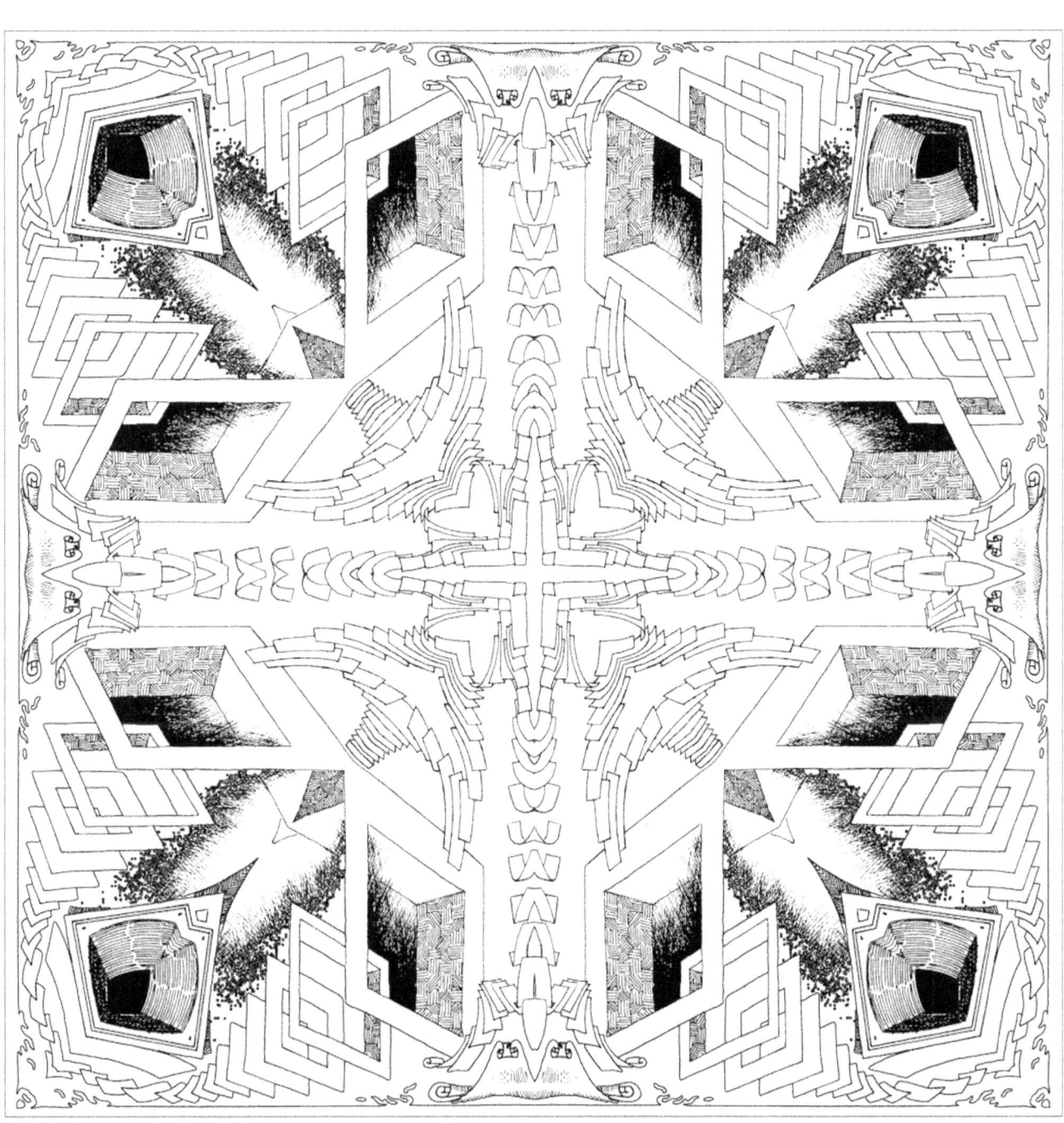

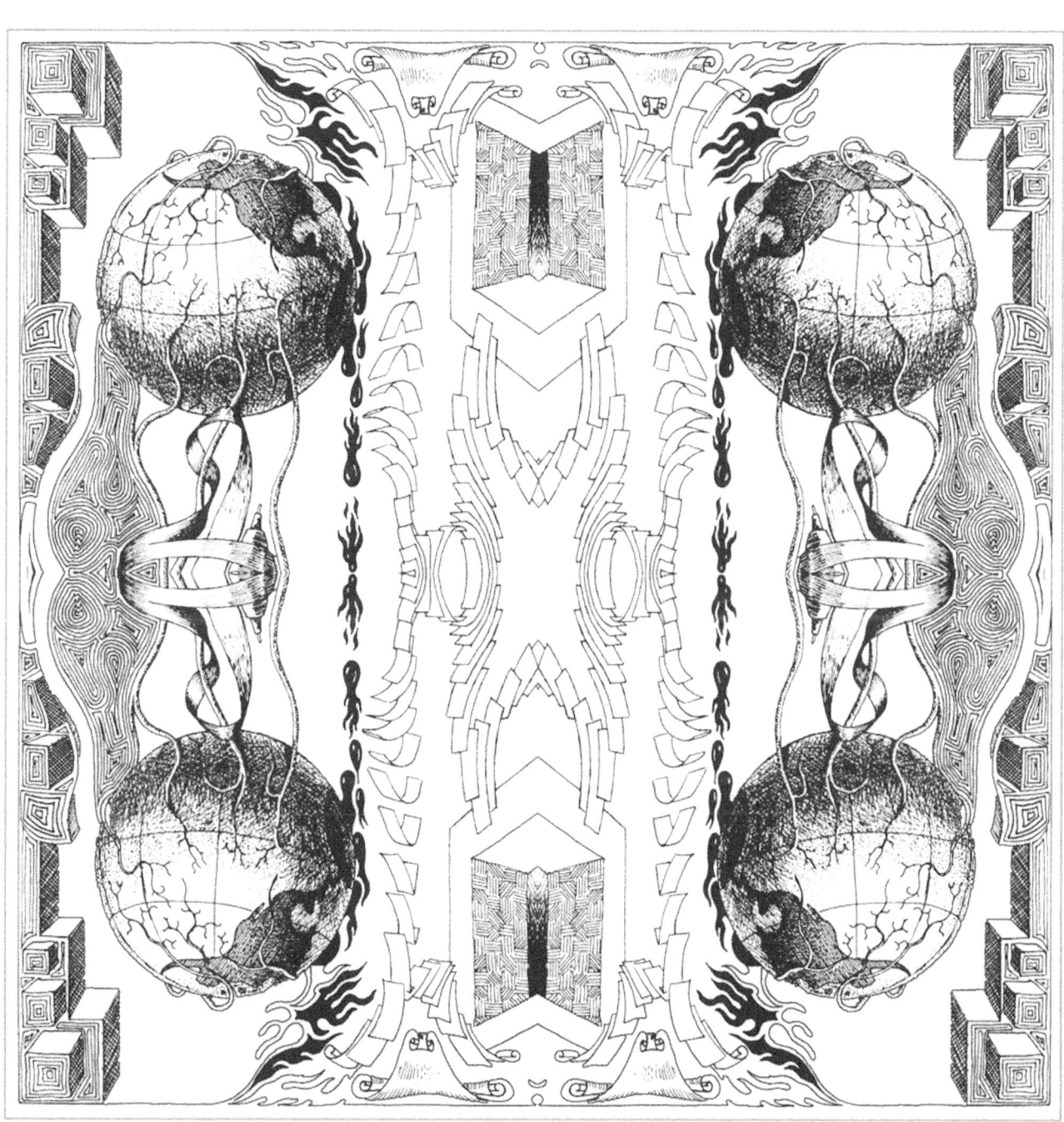

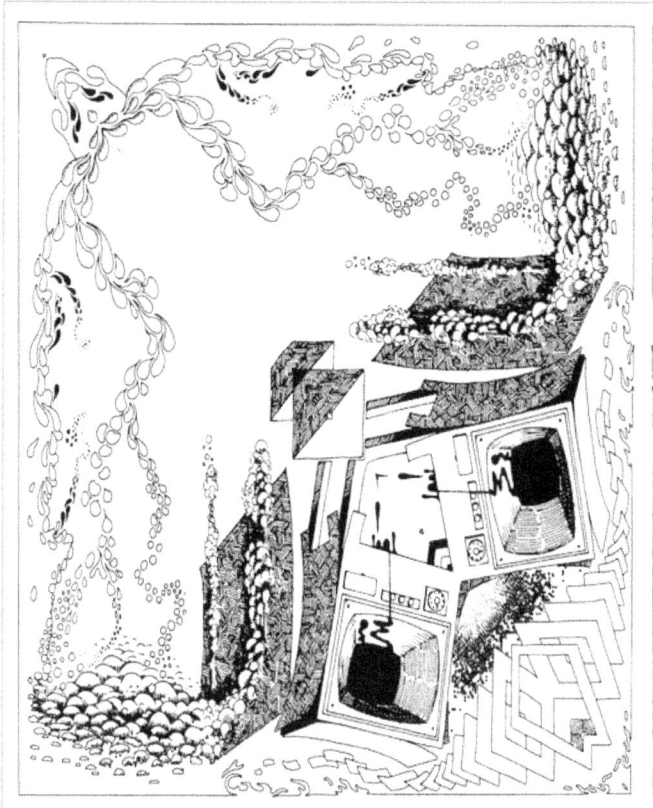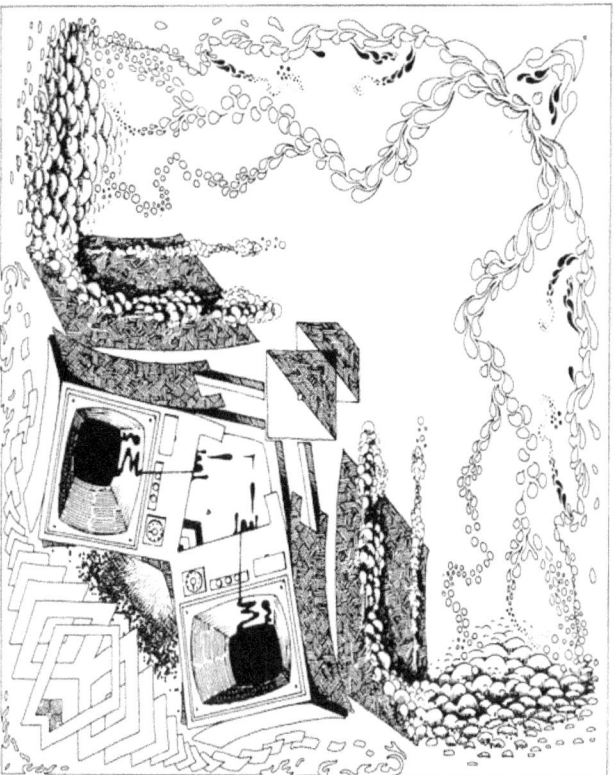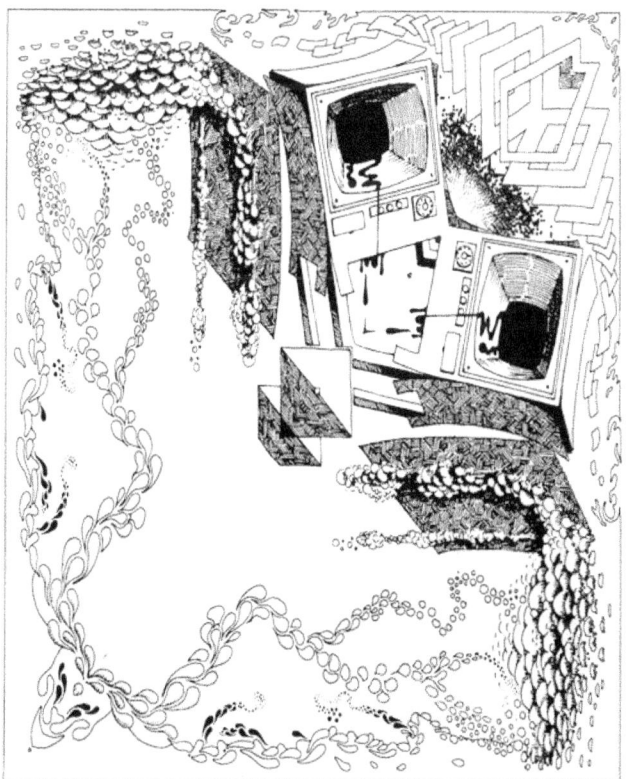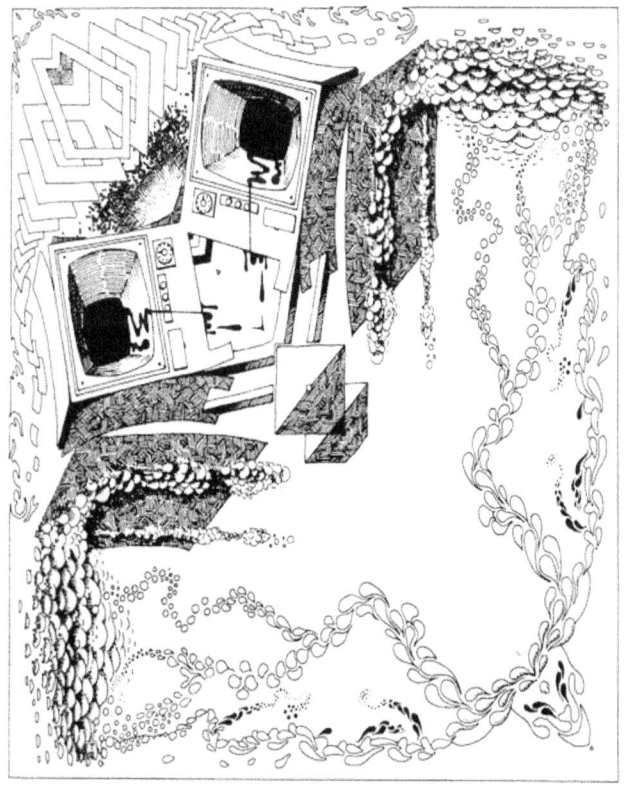

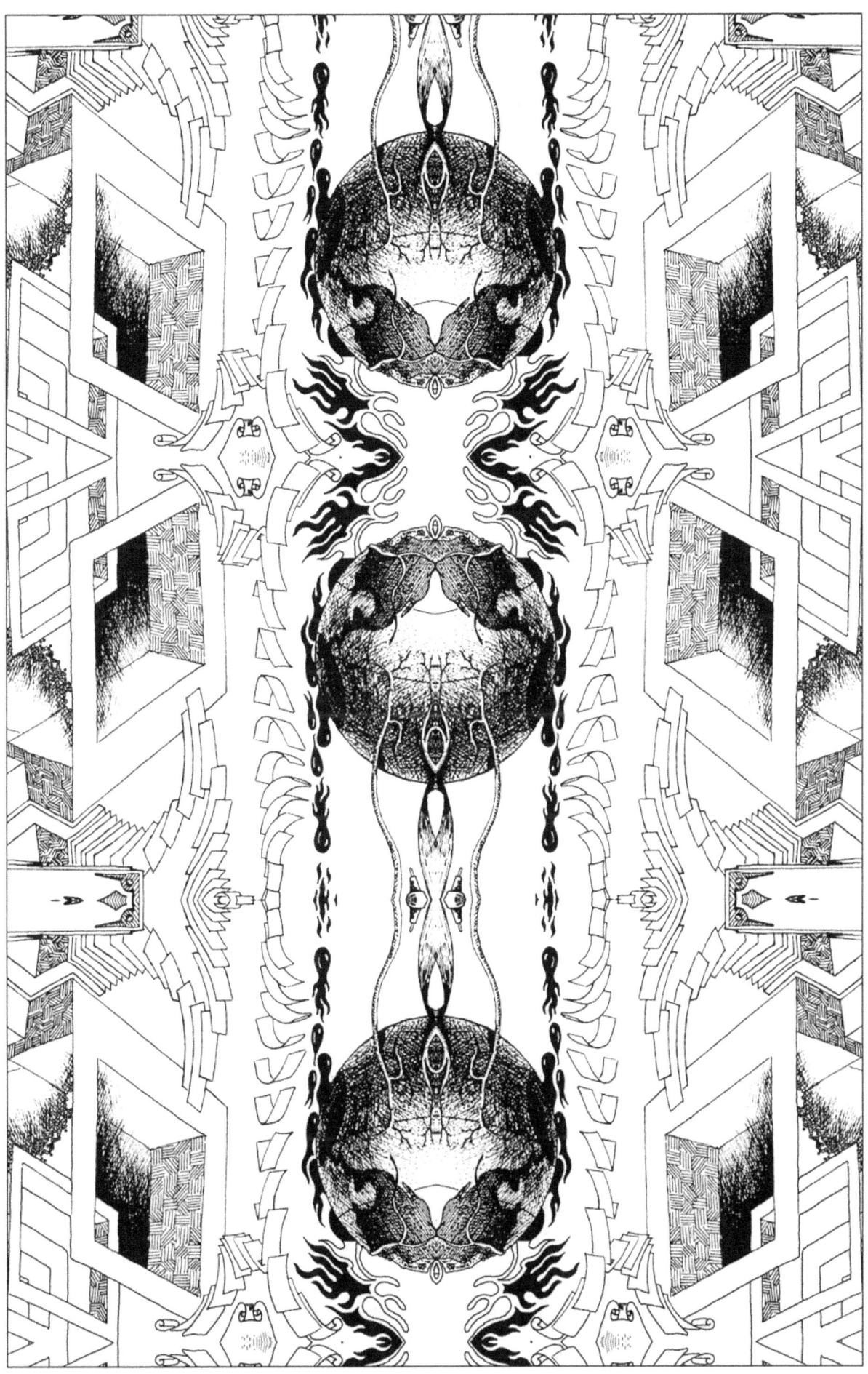

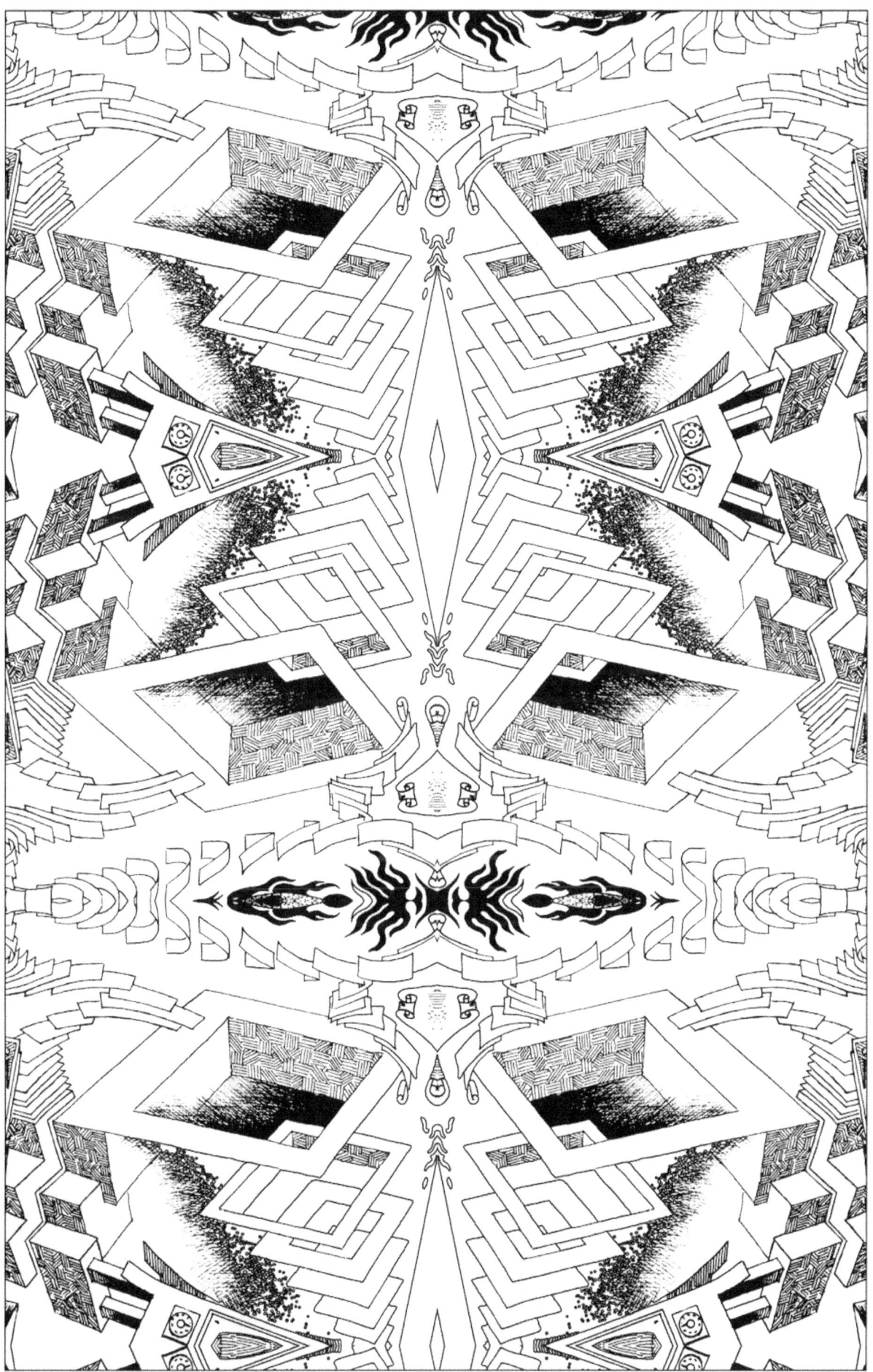

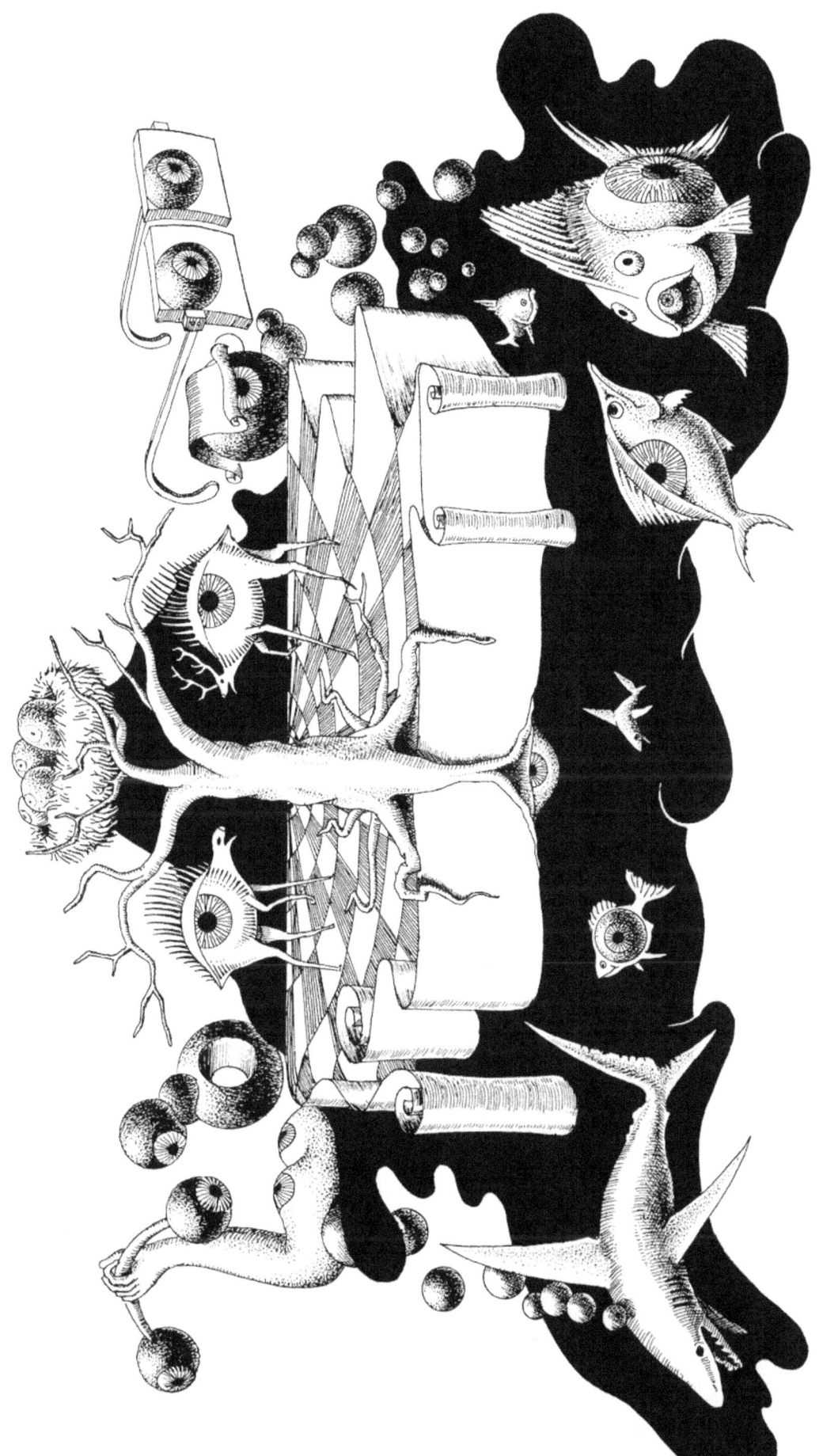

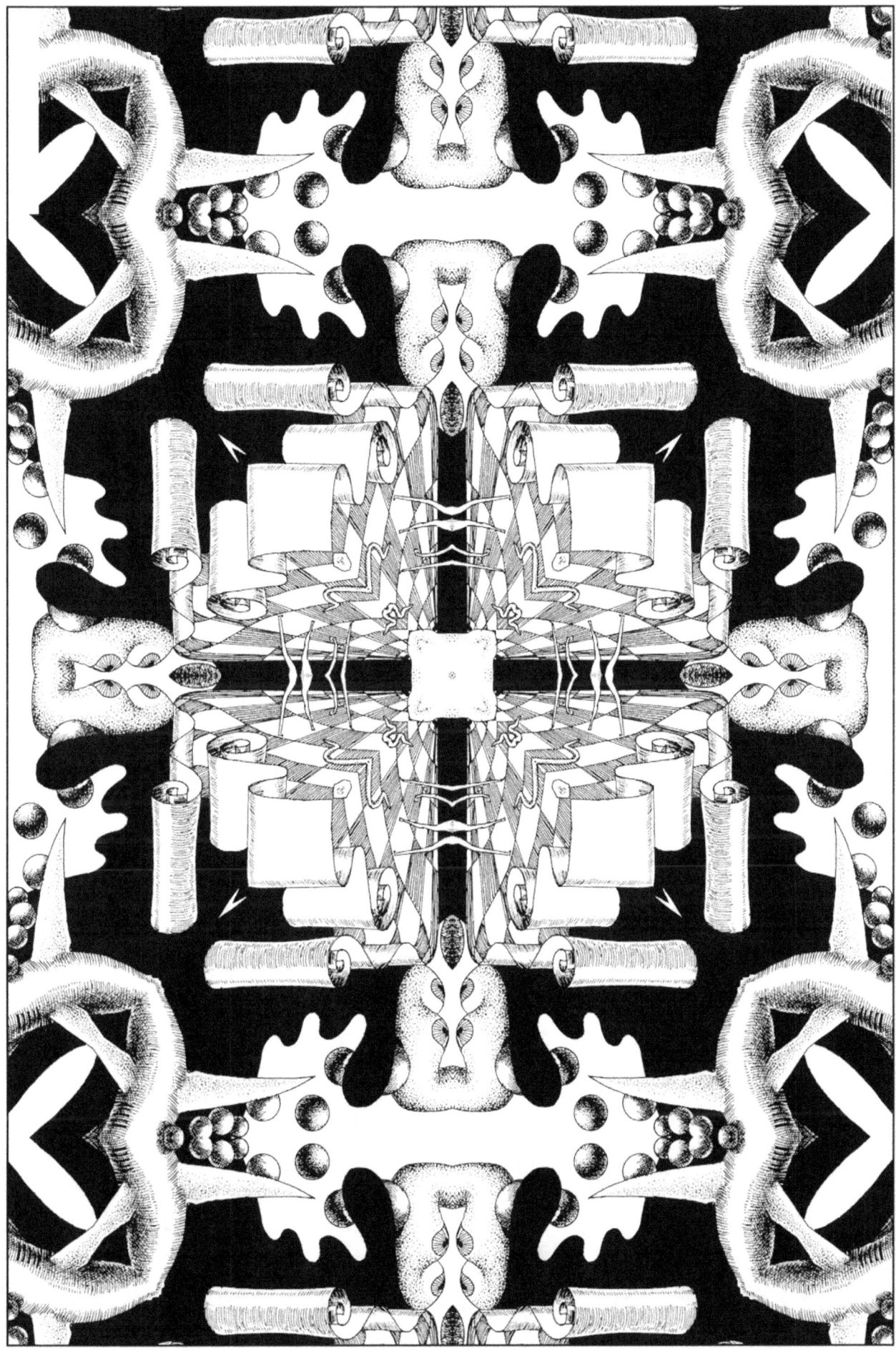

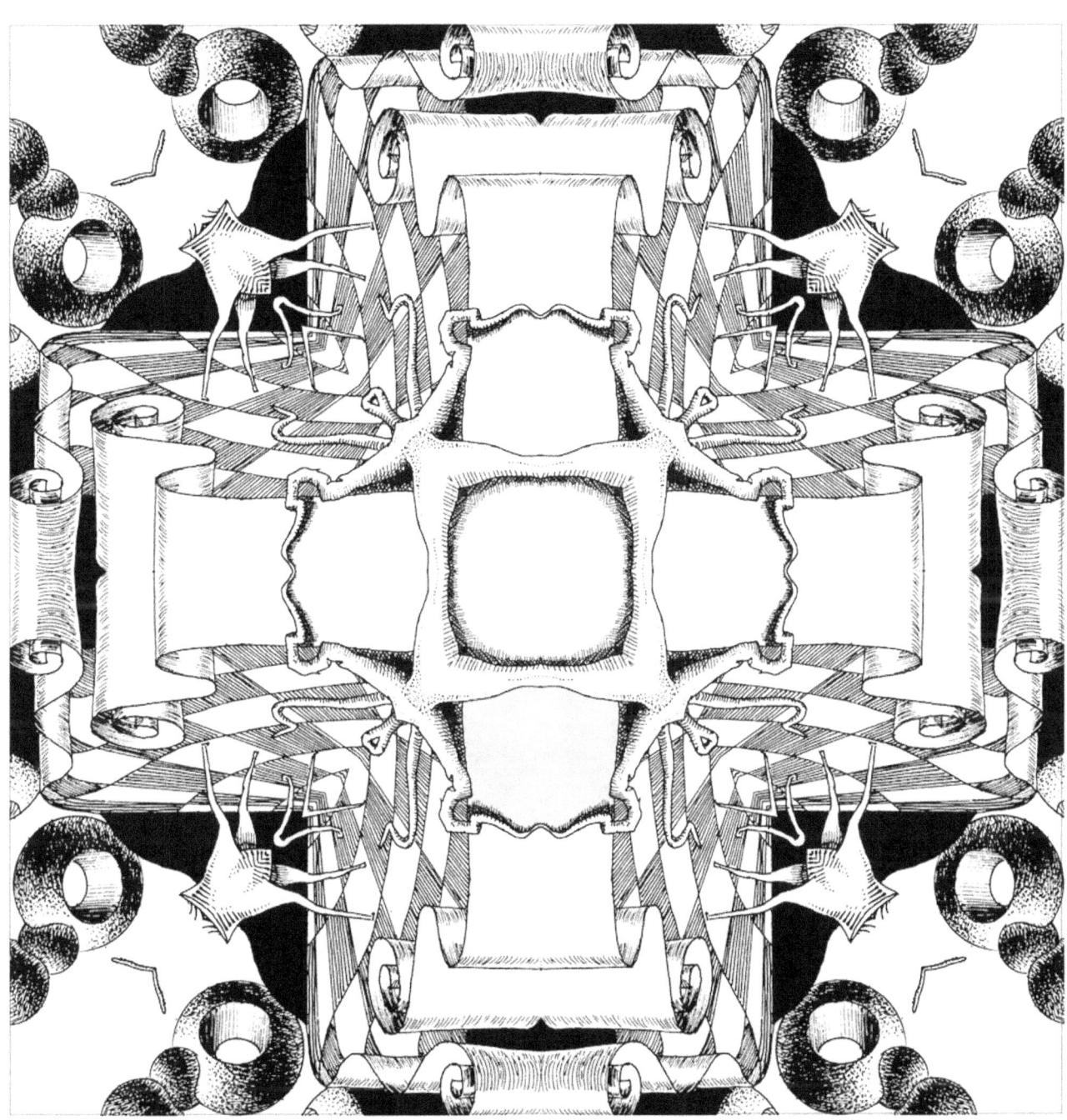

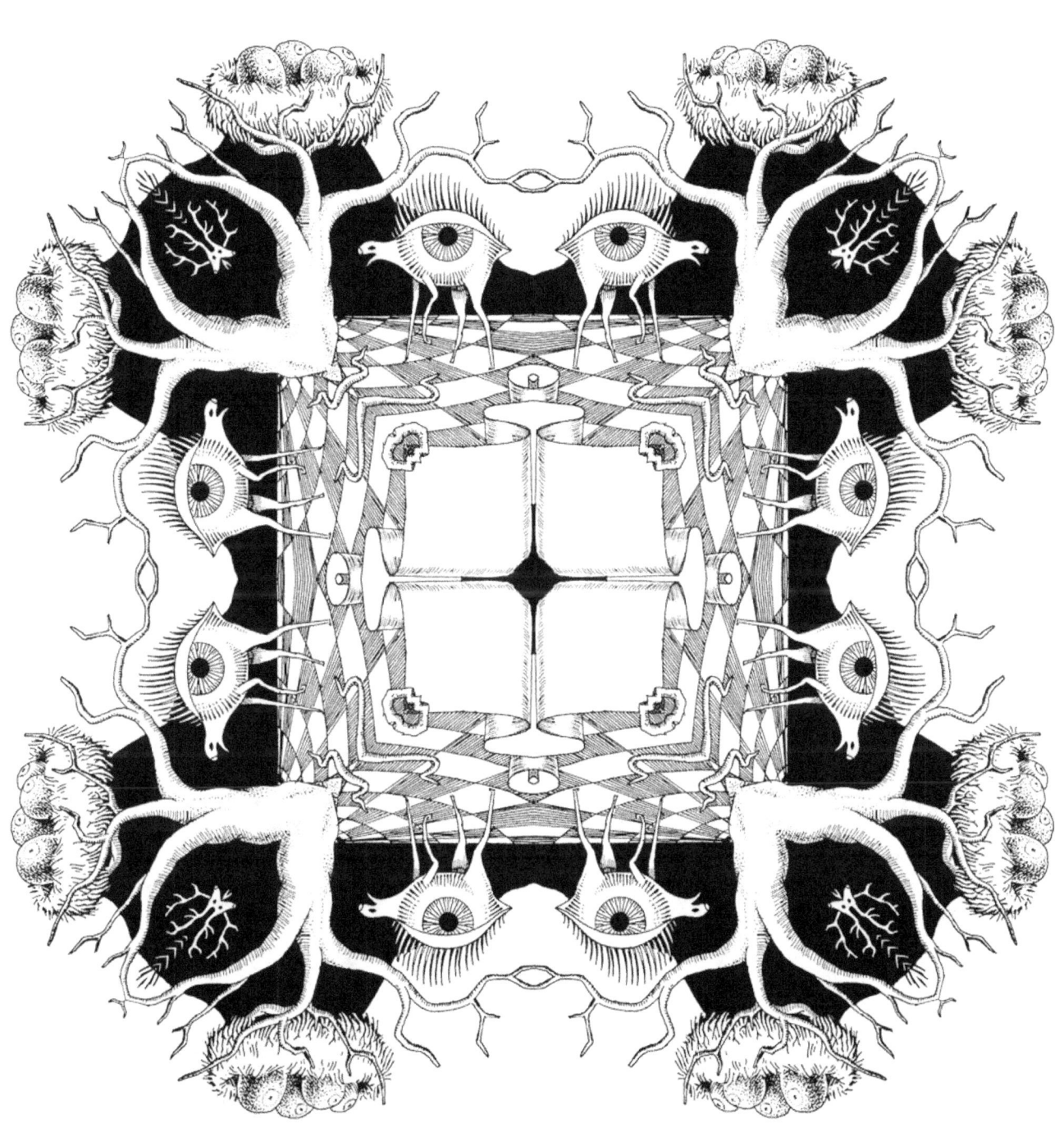

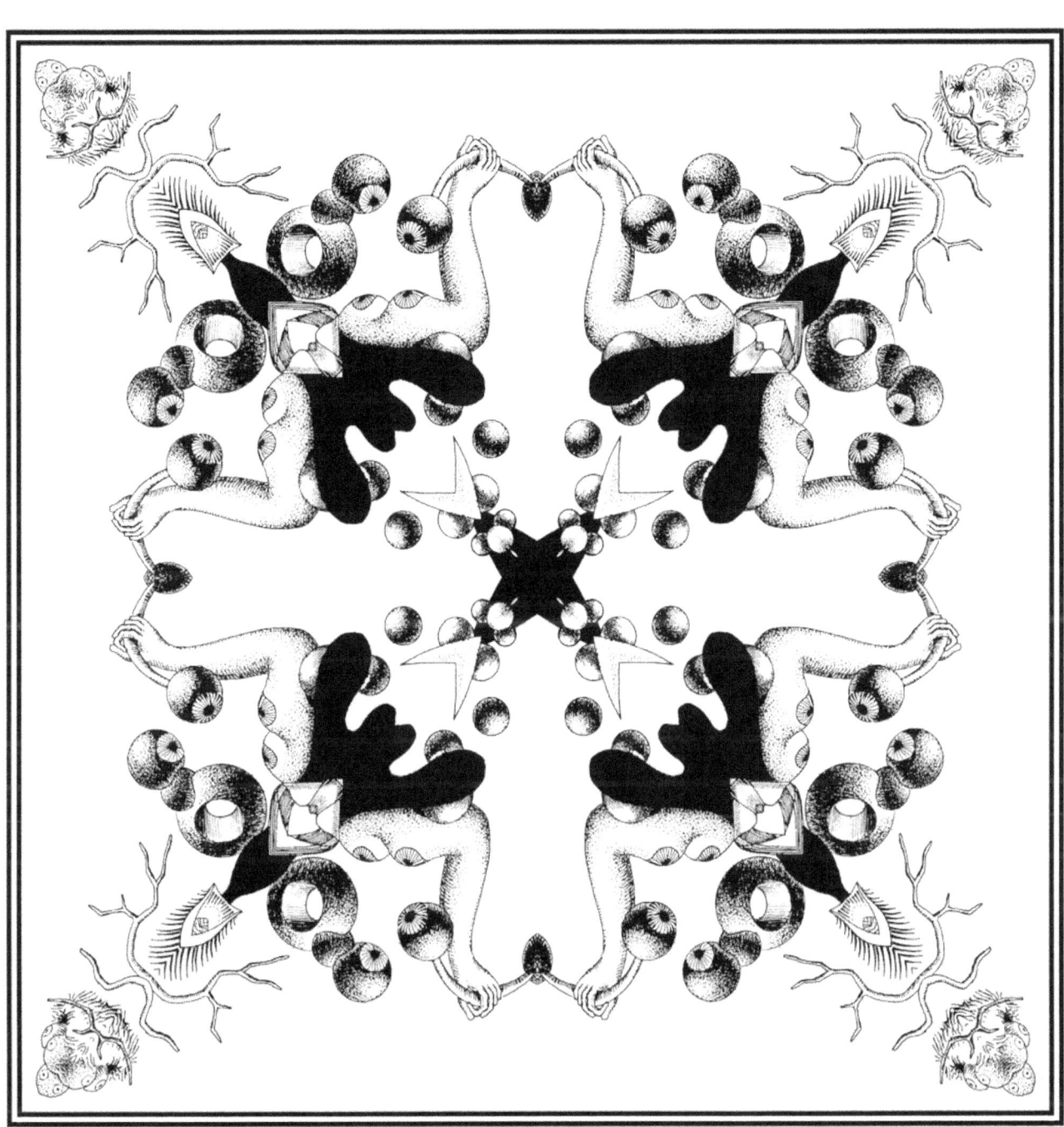

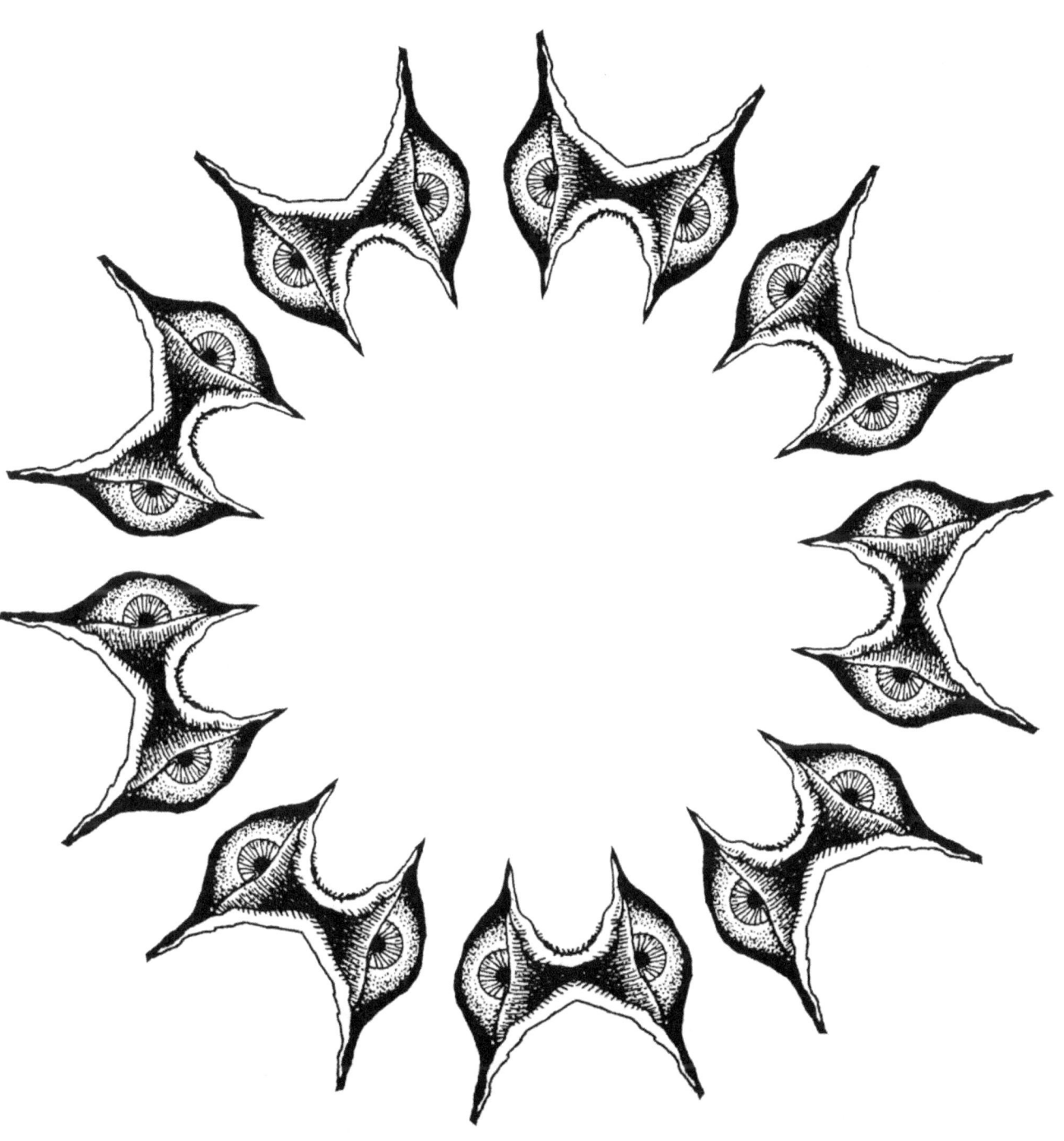

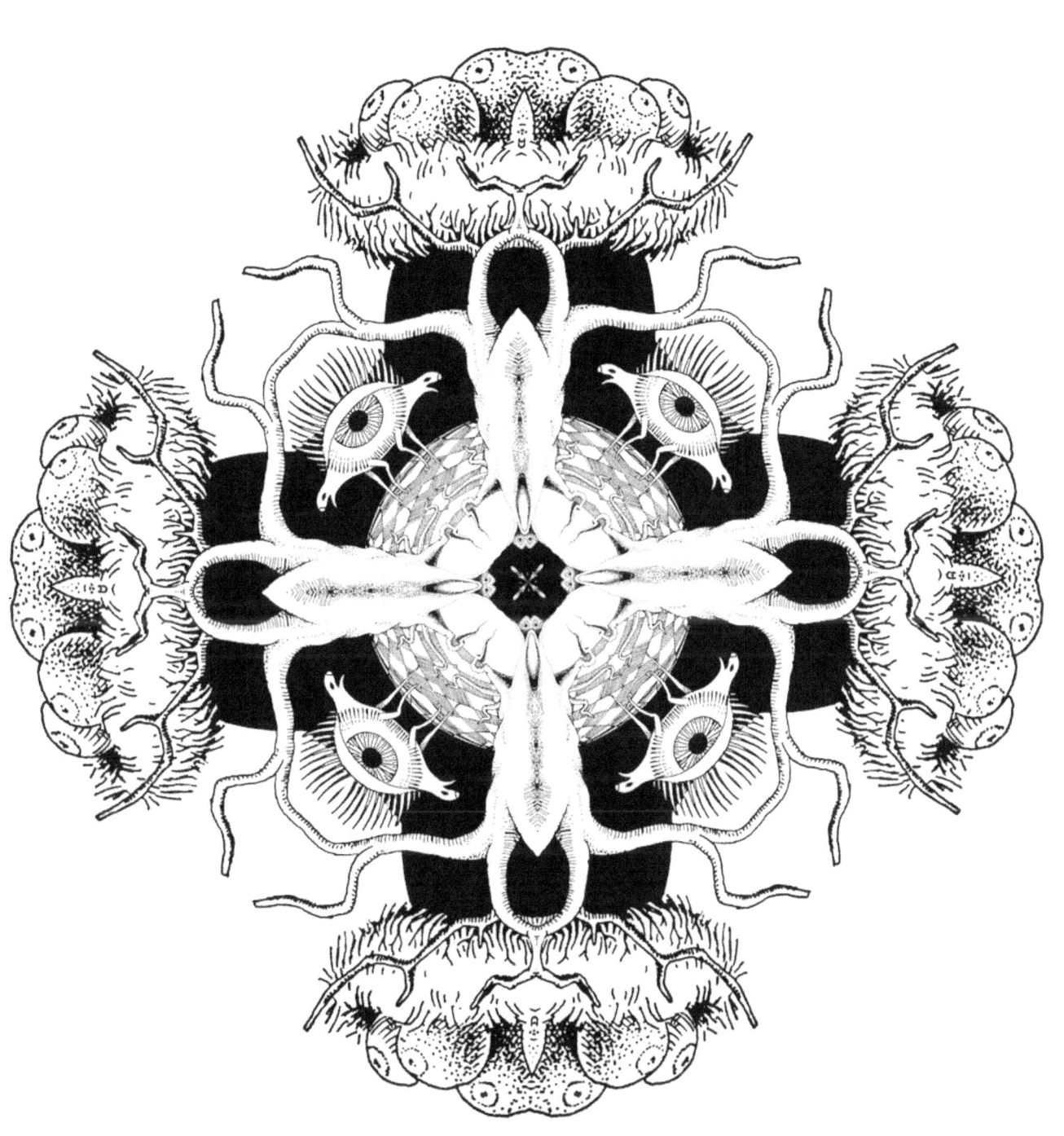

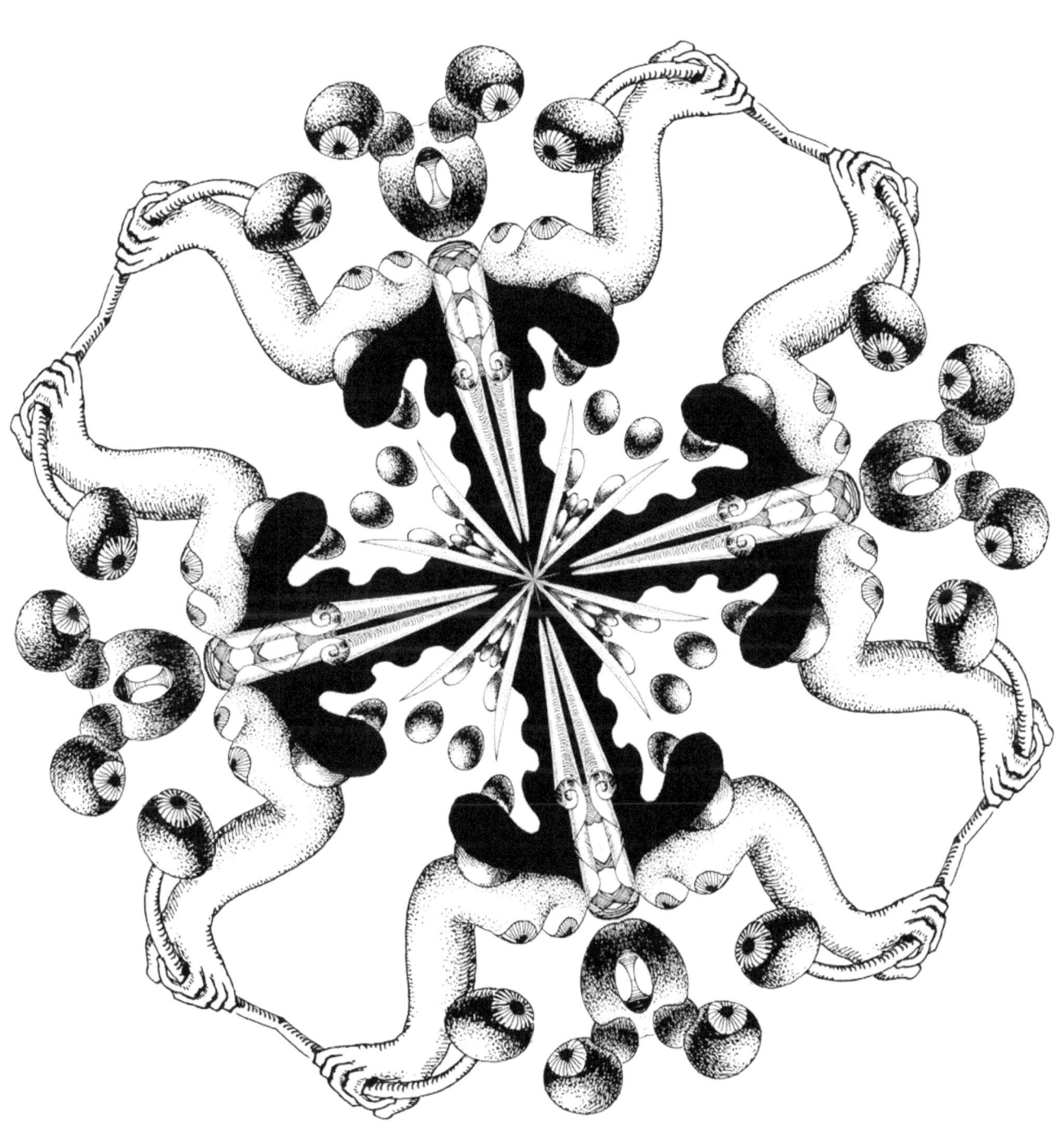

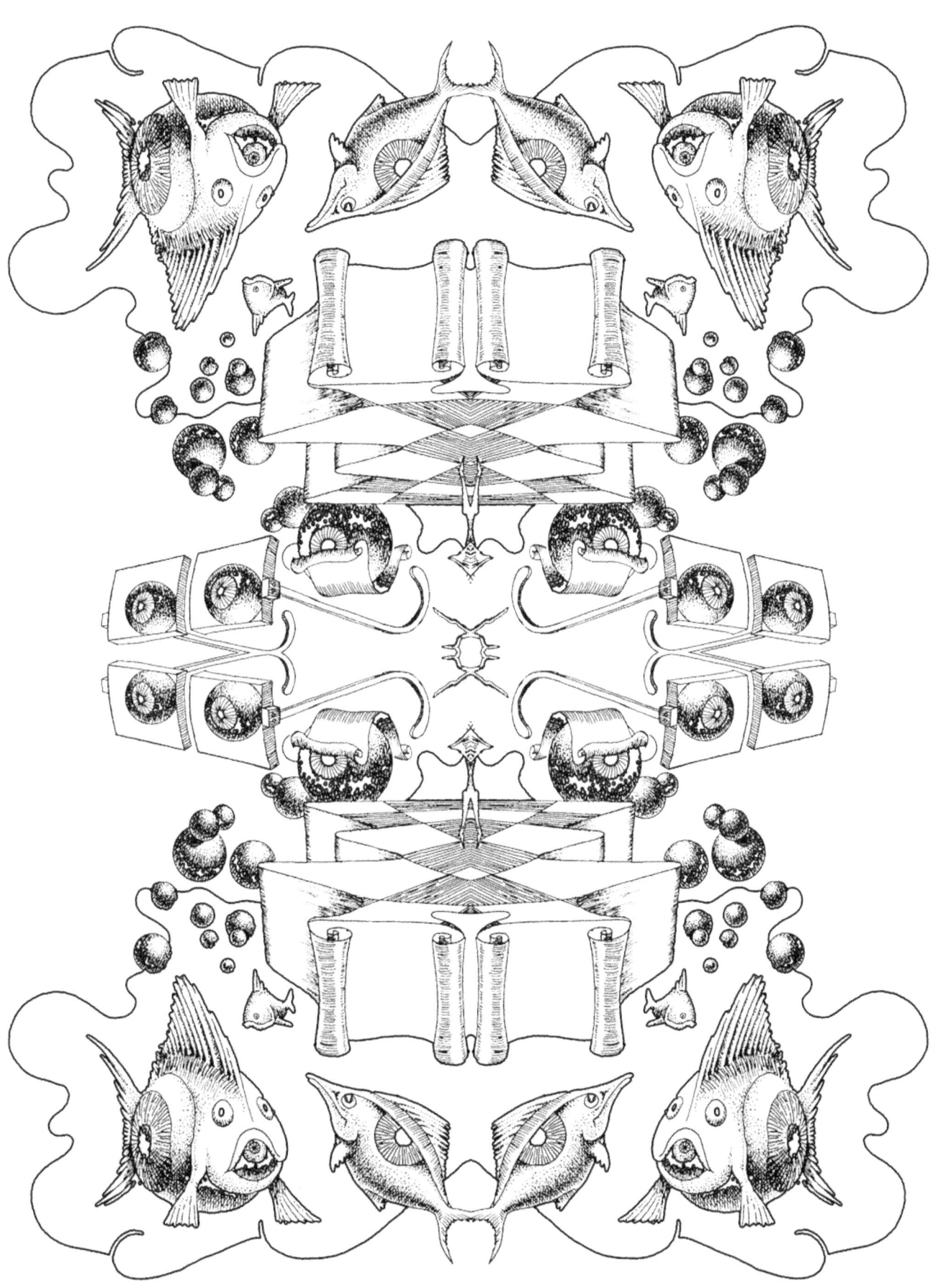

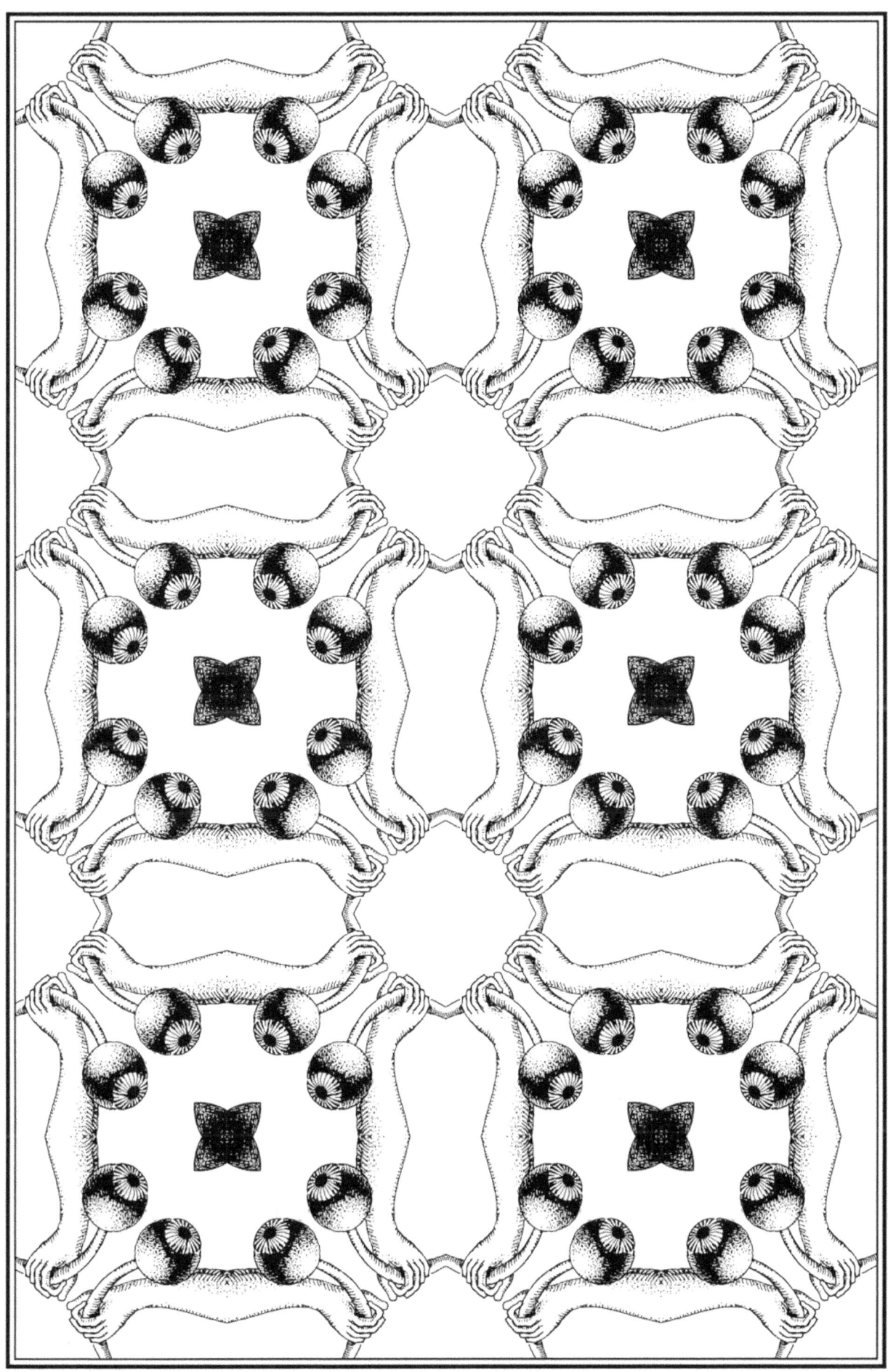

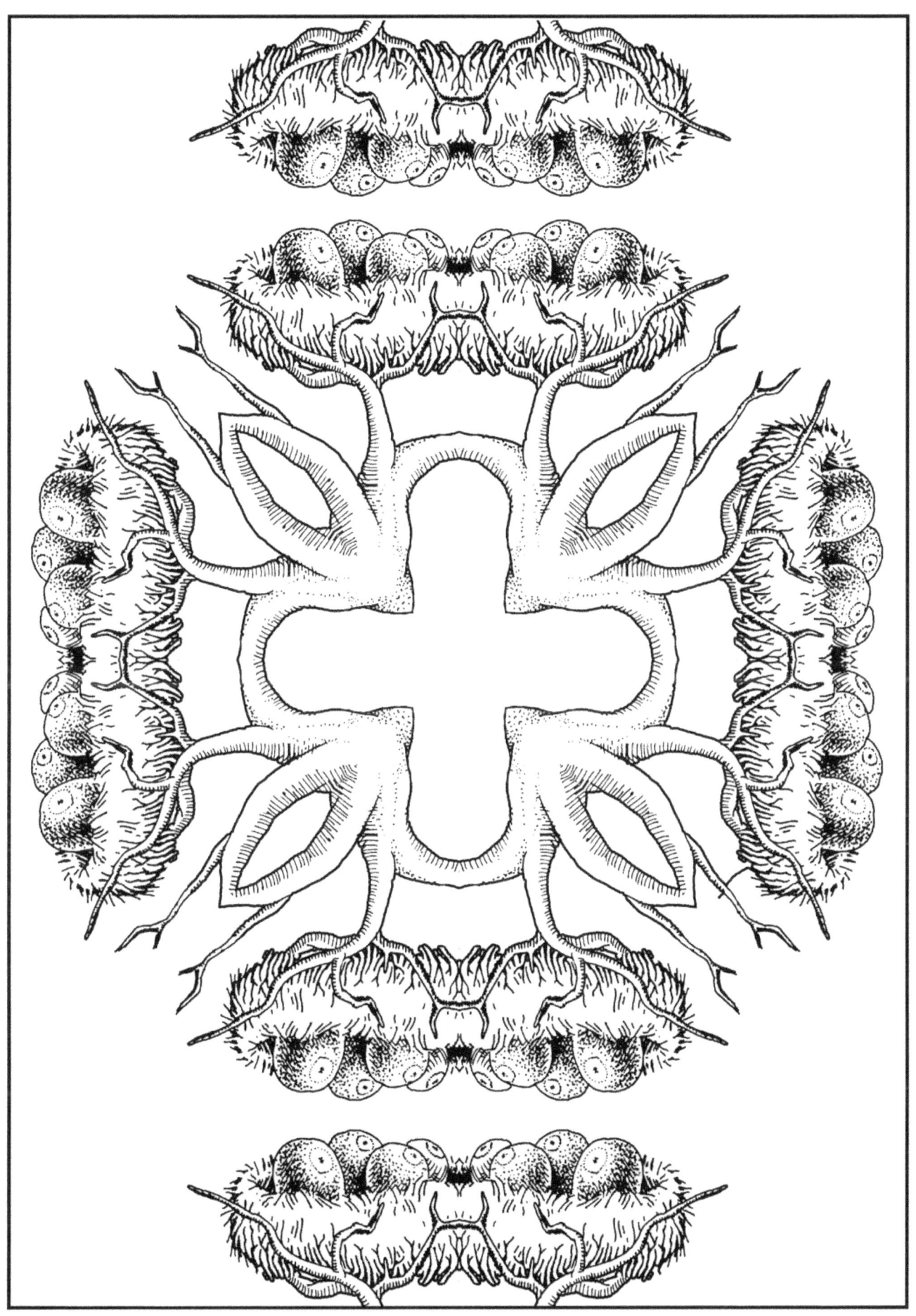

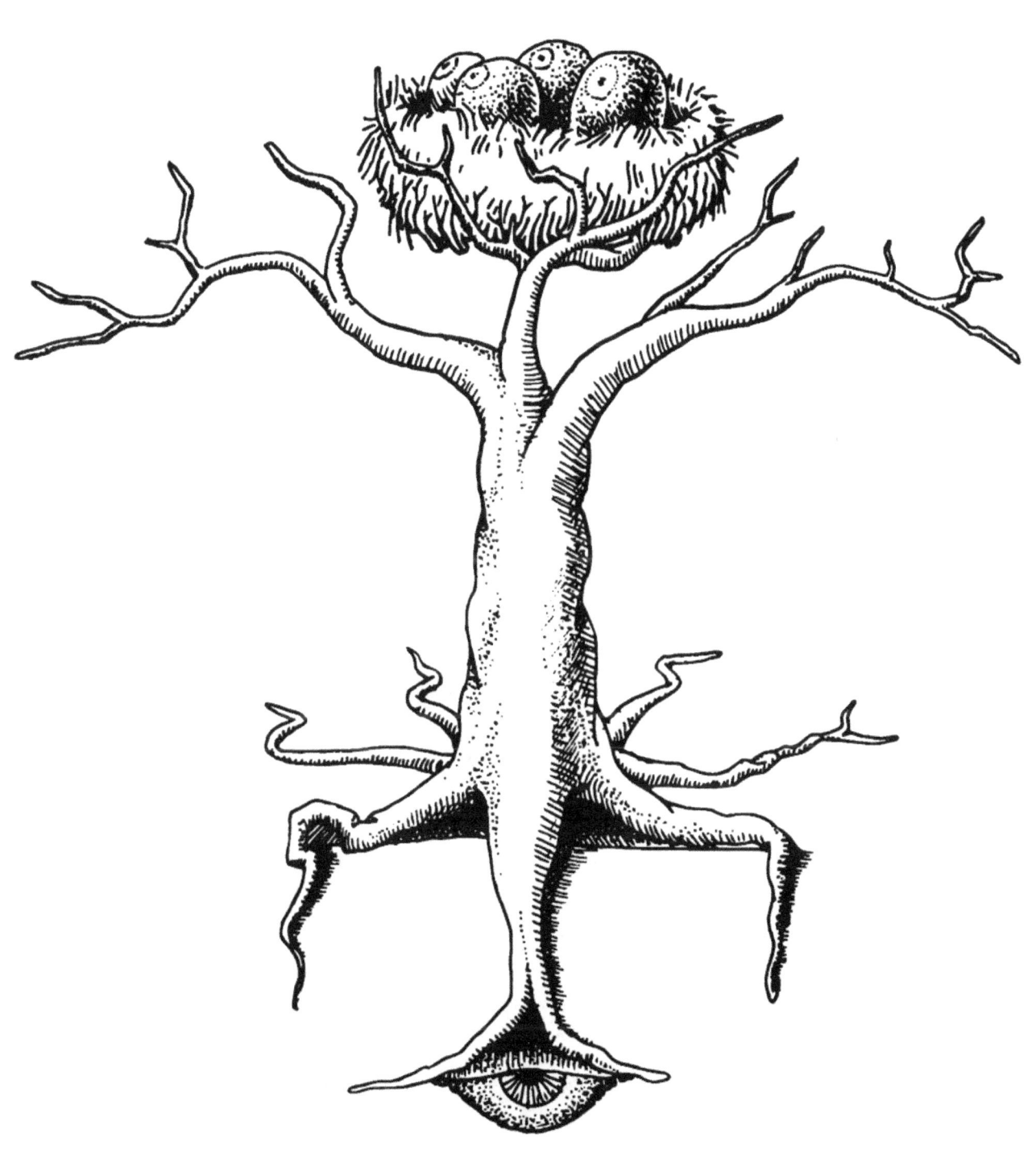

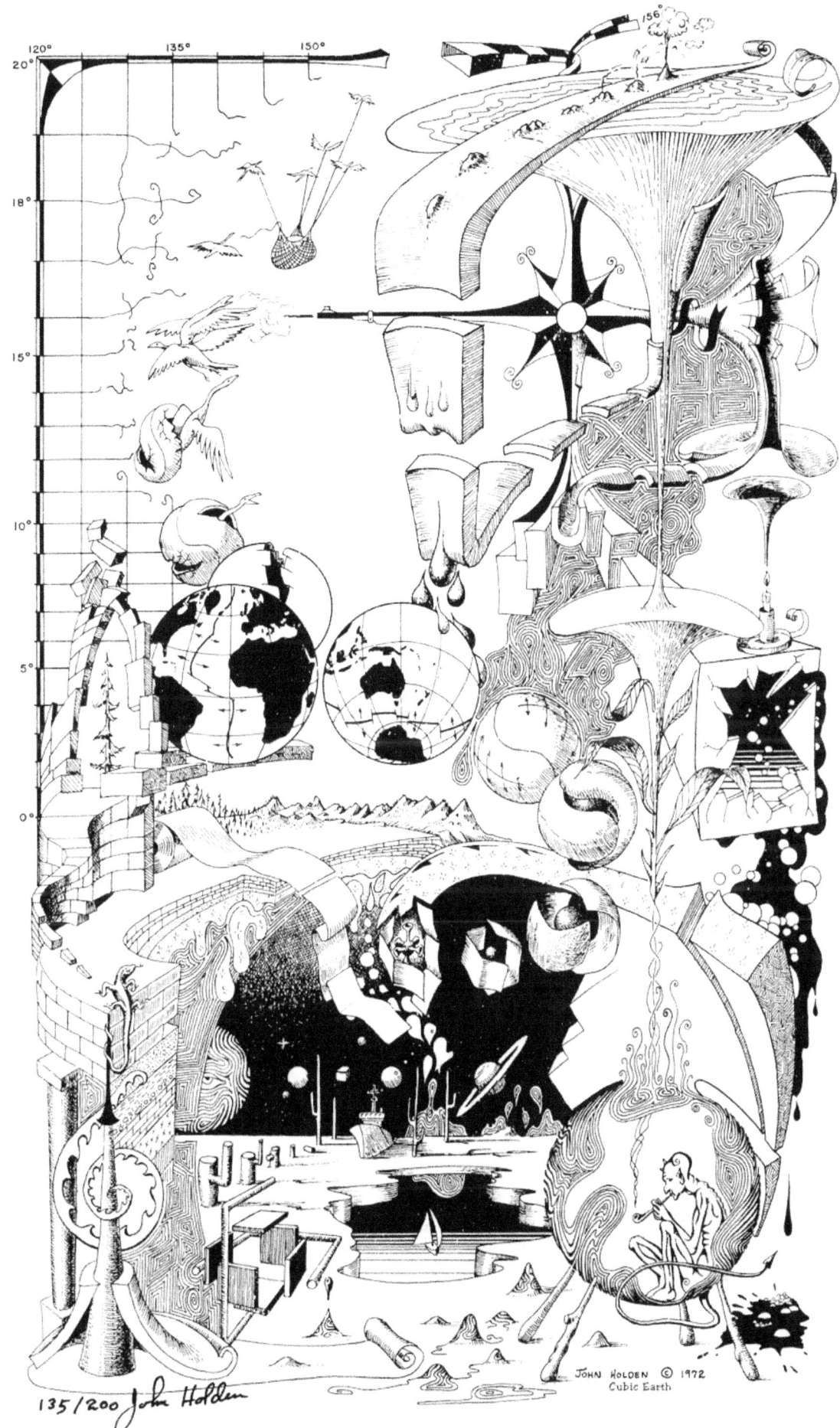

135/200 John Holden

JOHN HOLDEN © 1972
Cubic Earth

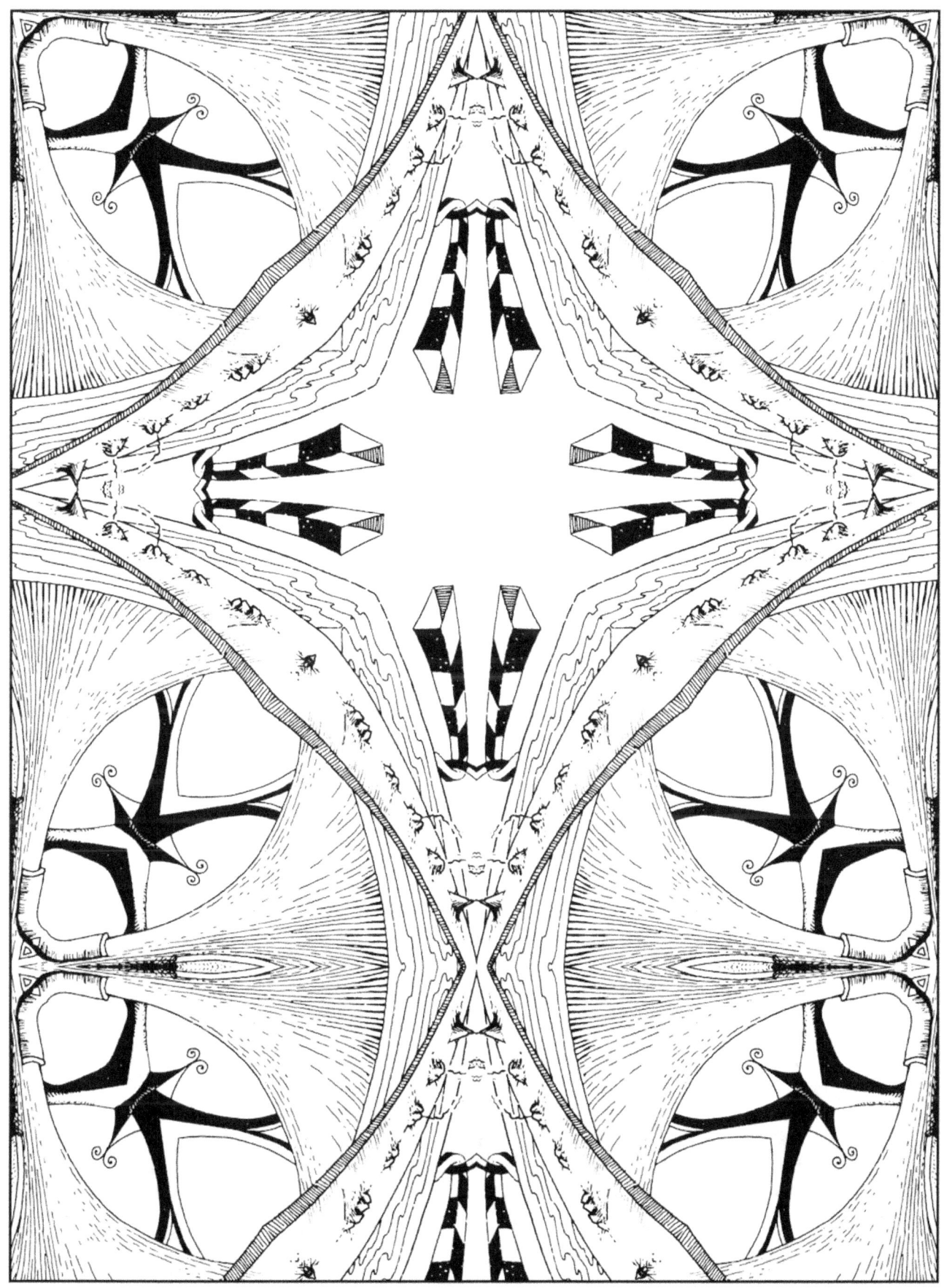

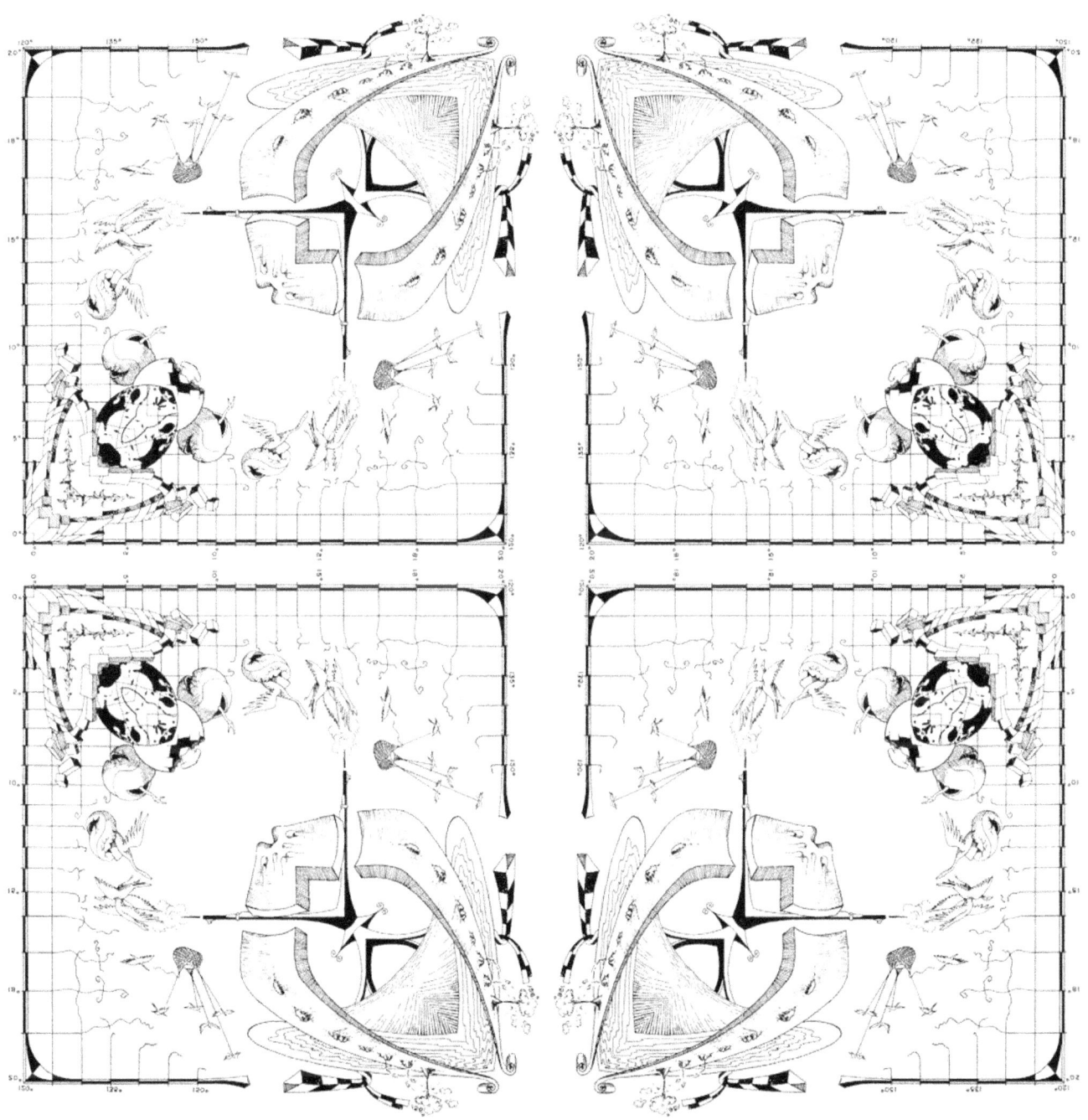

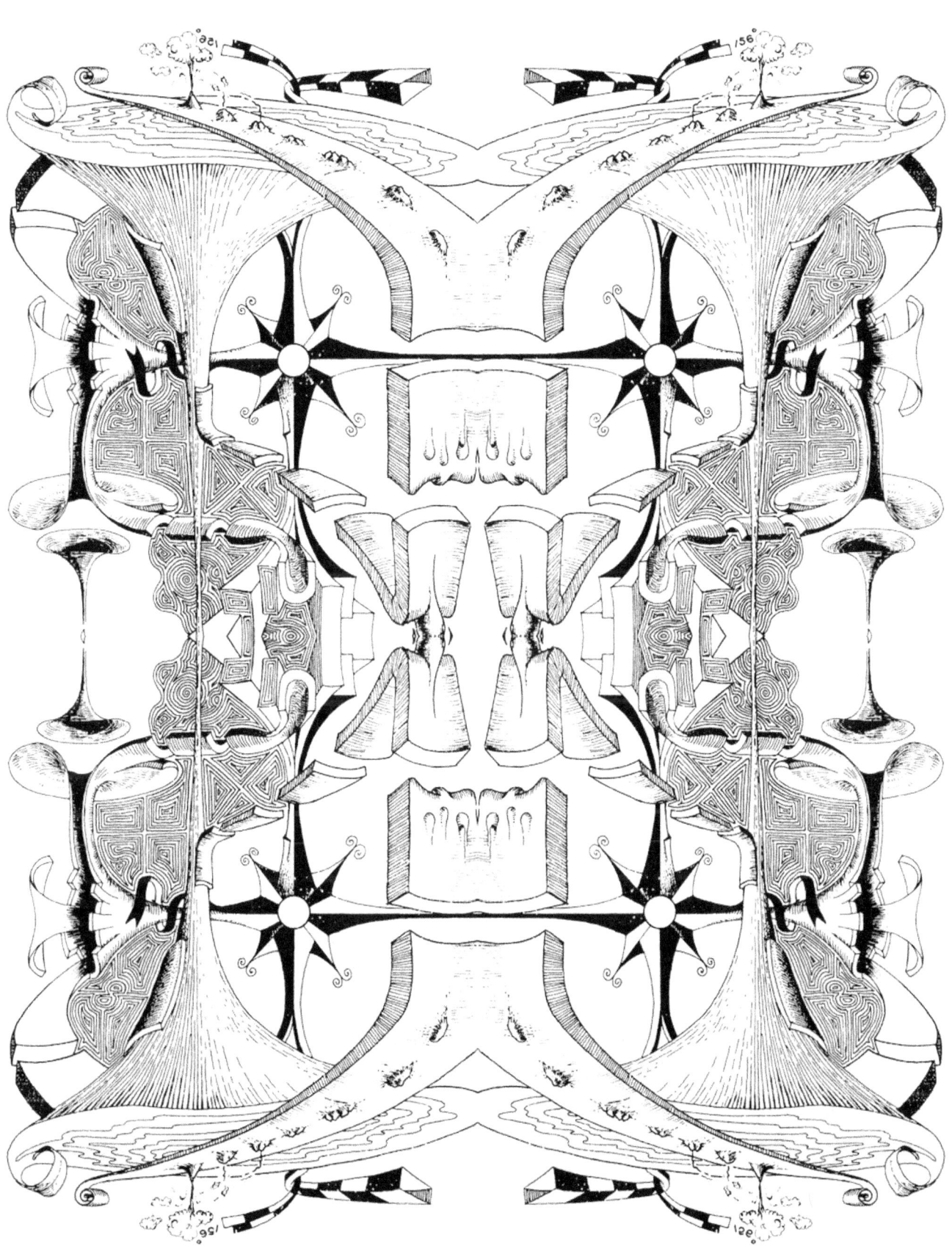

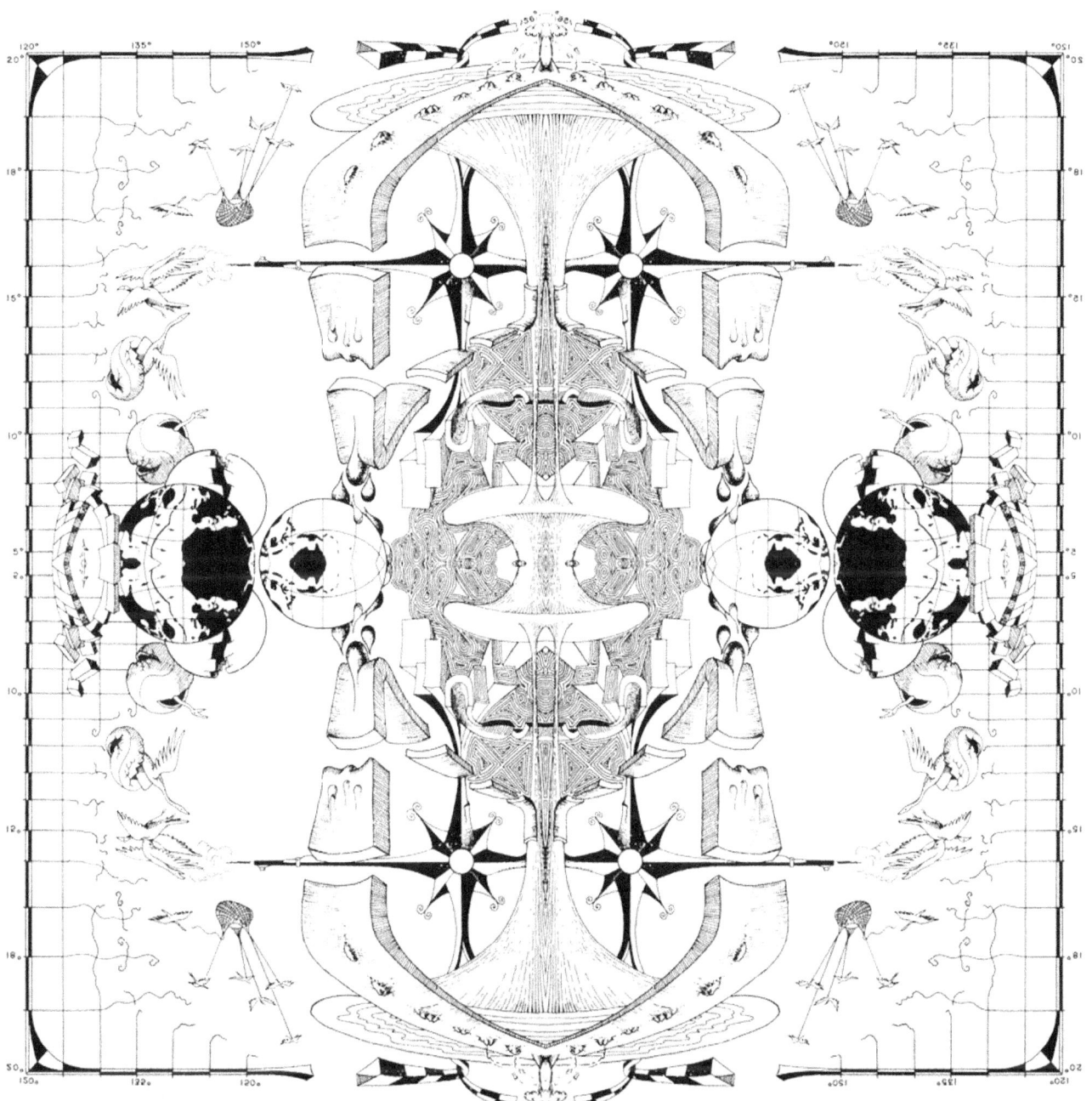

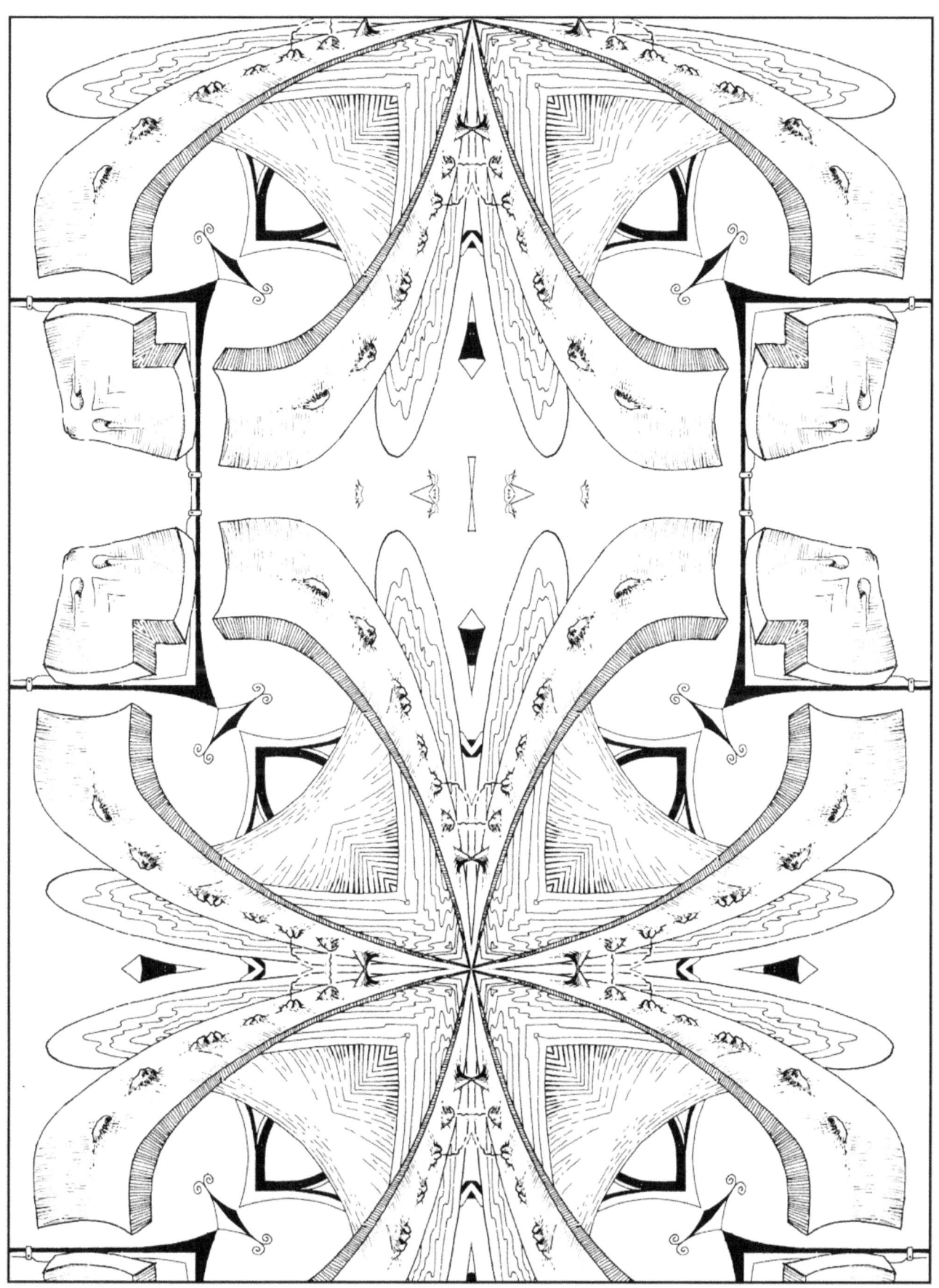

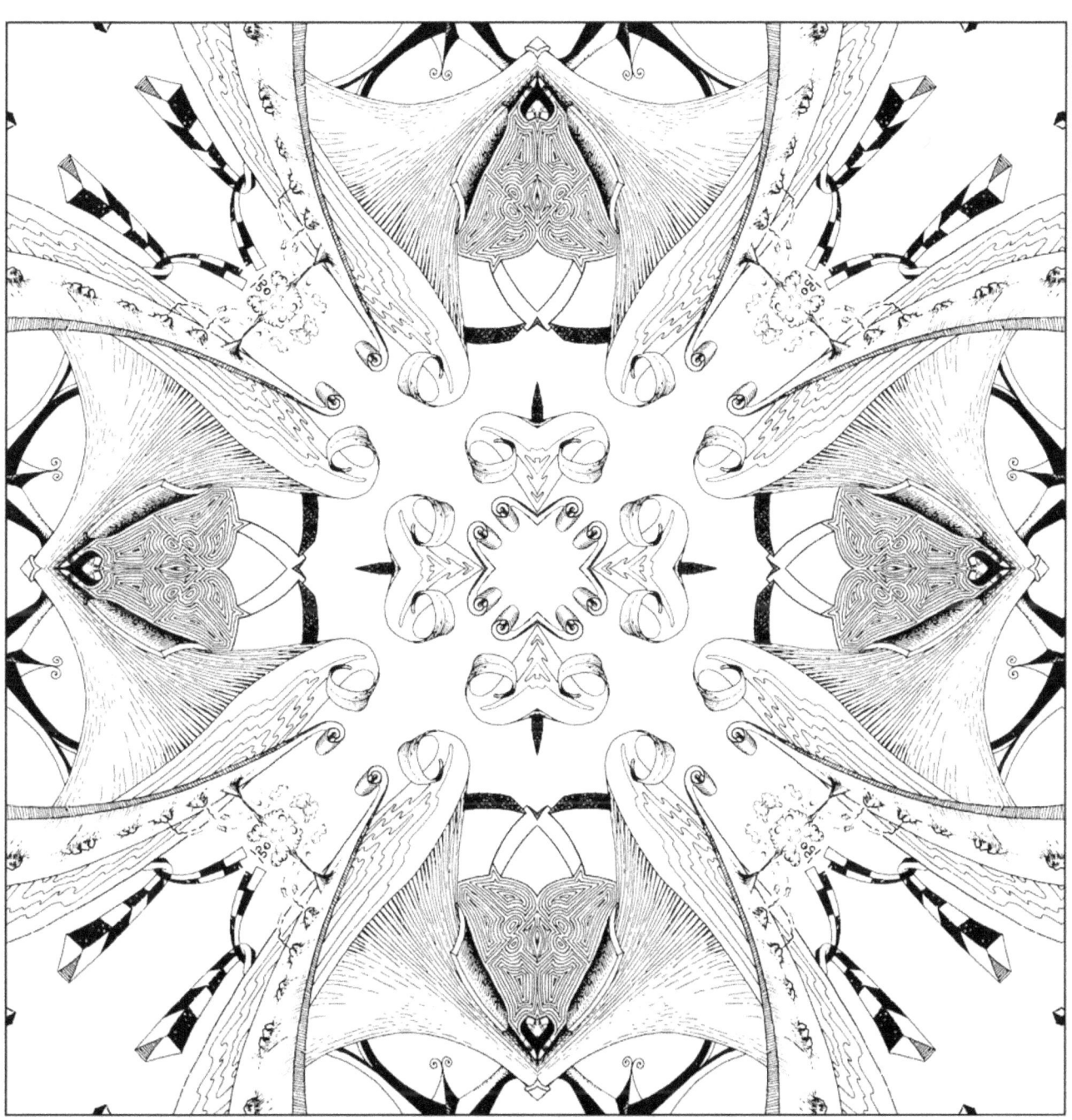

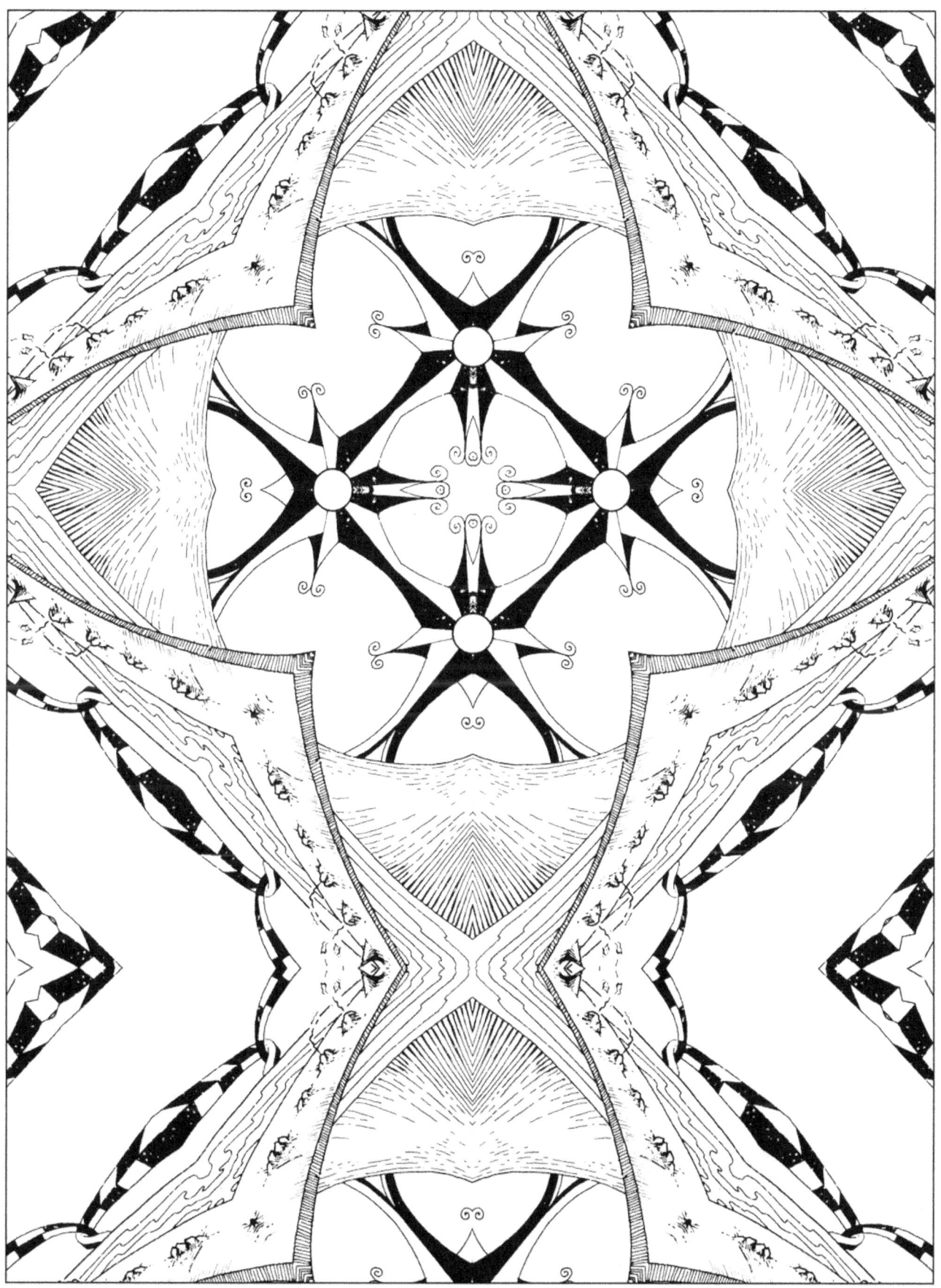

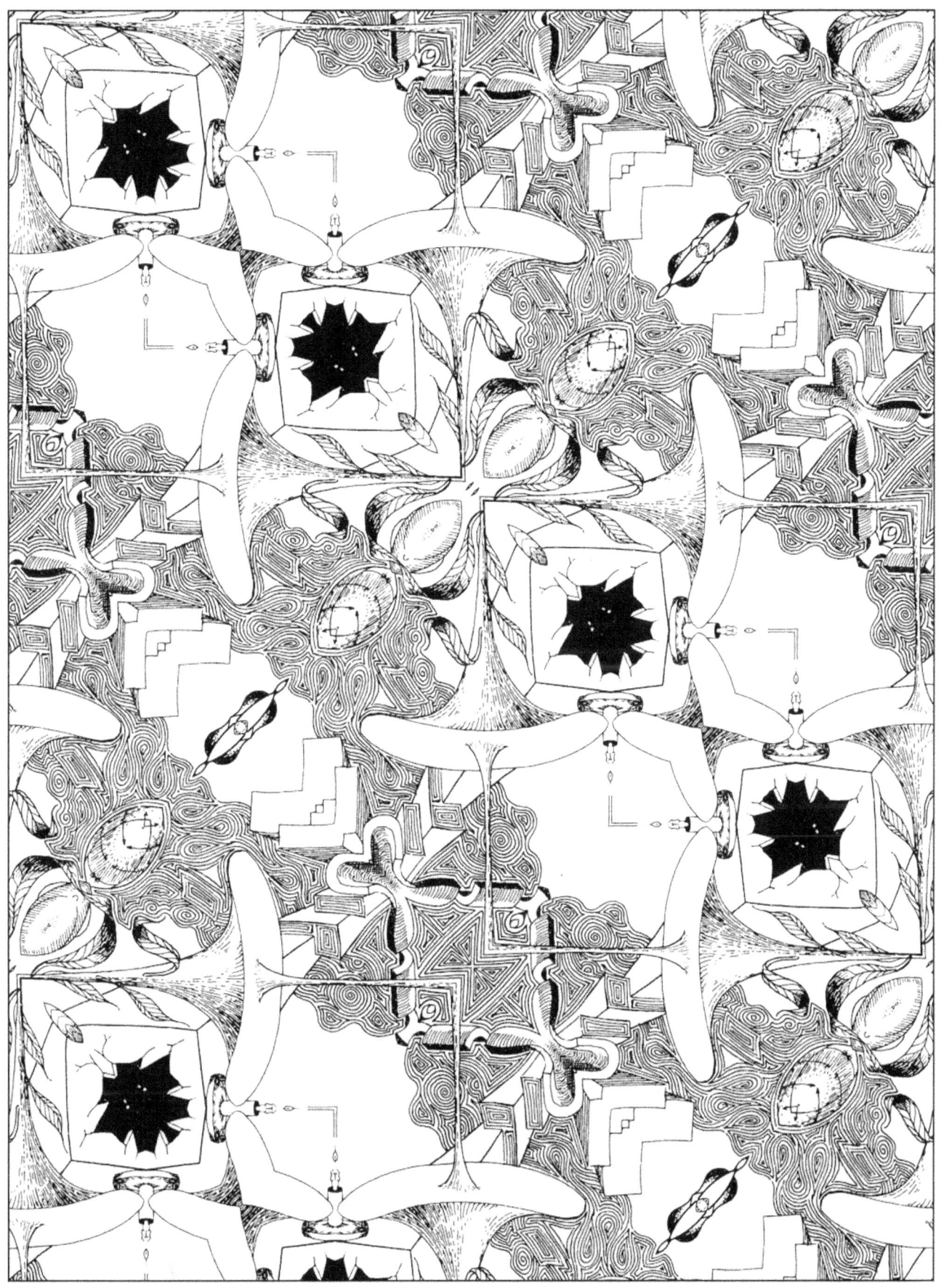

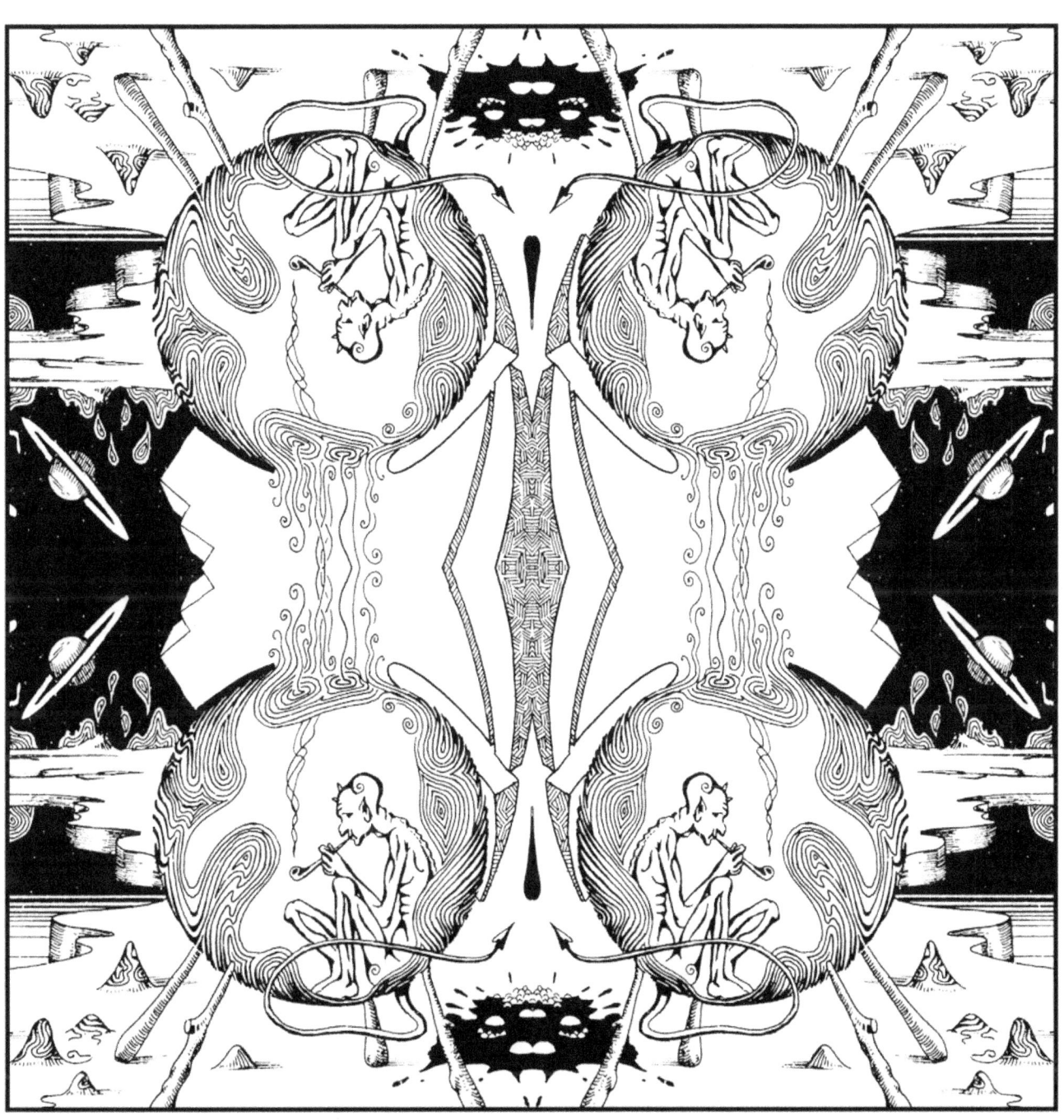

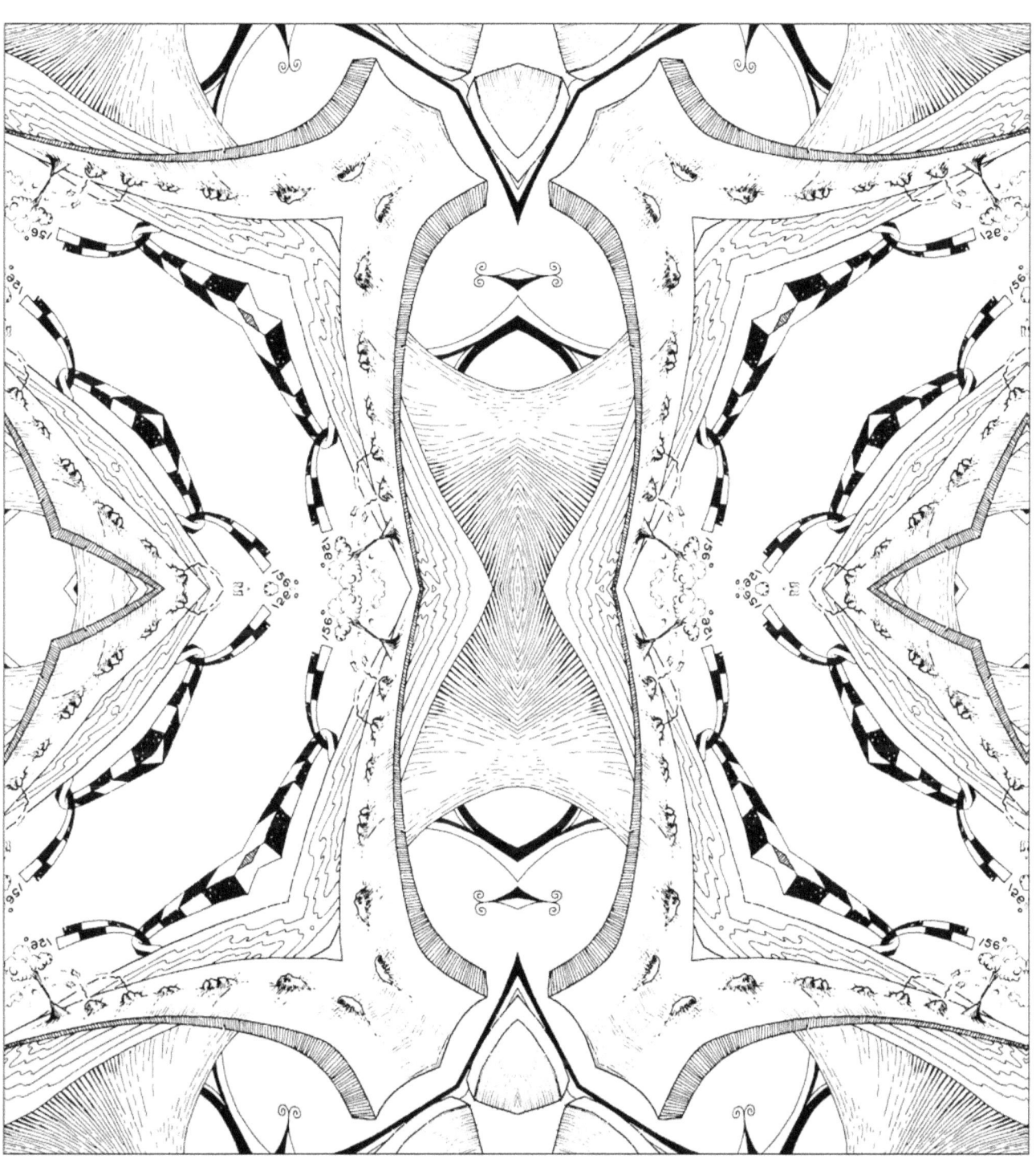

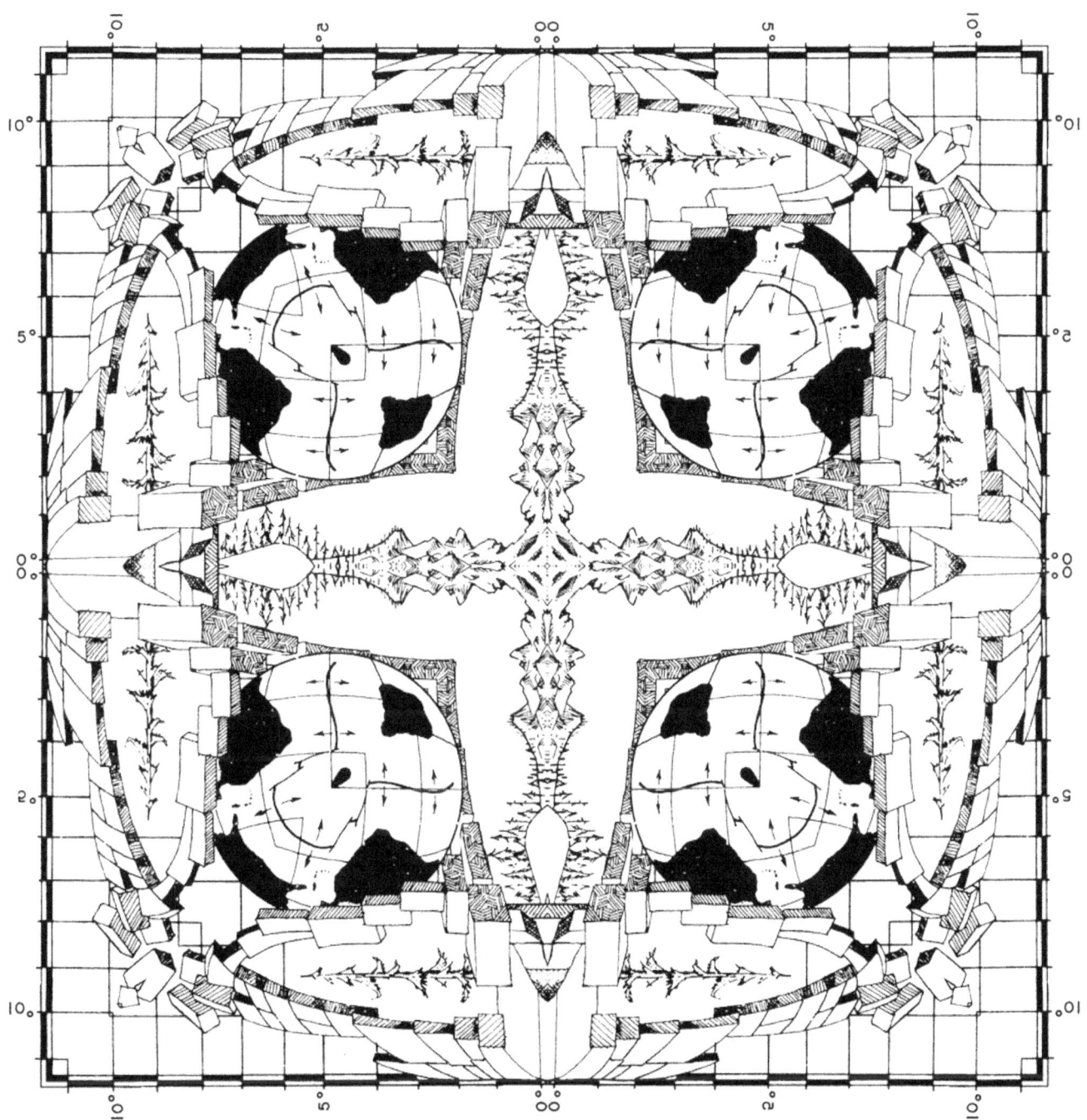

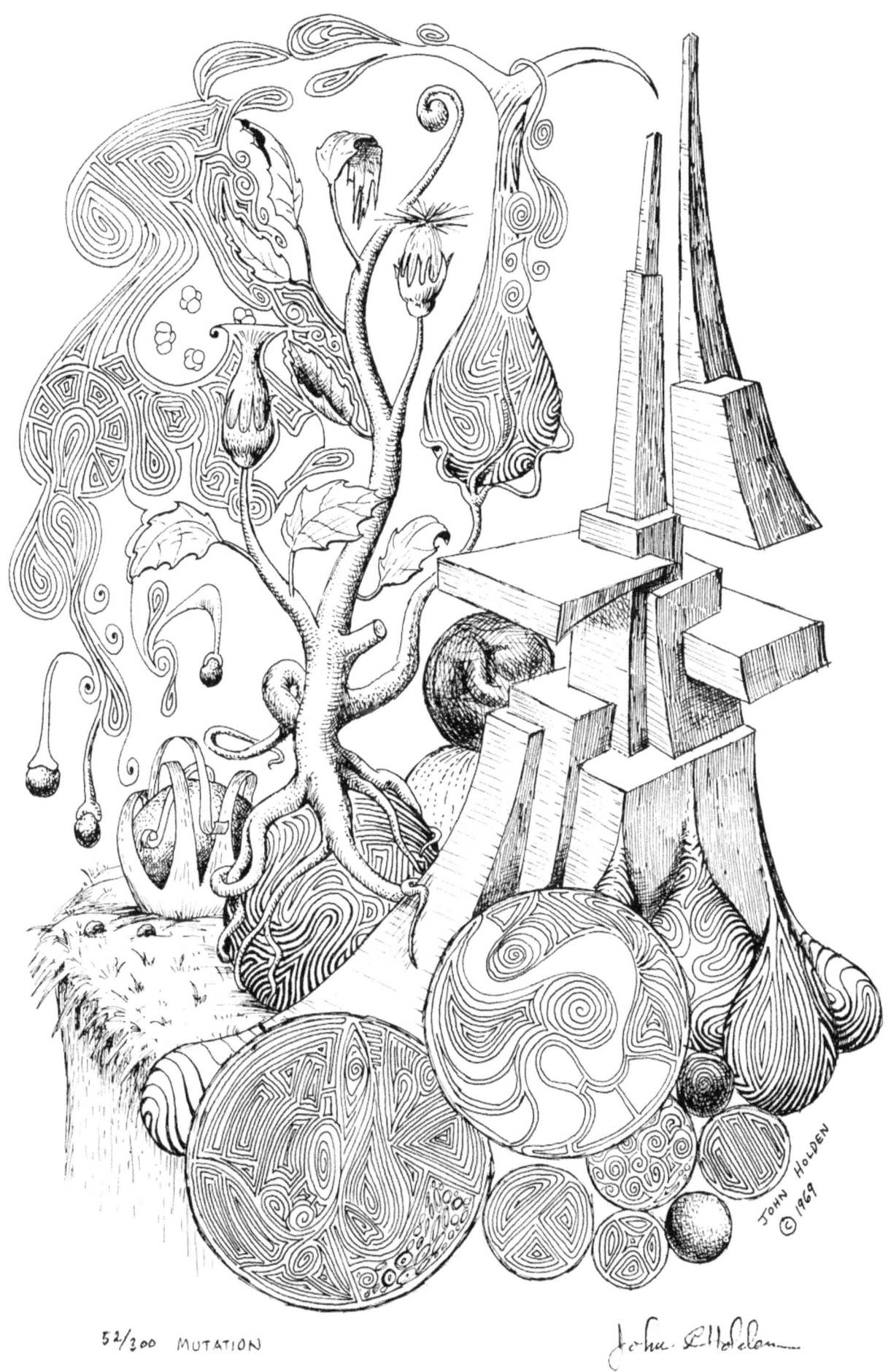

52/300 MUTATION

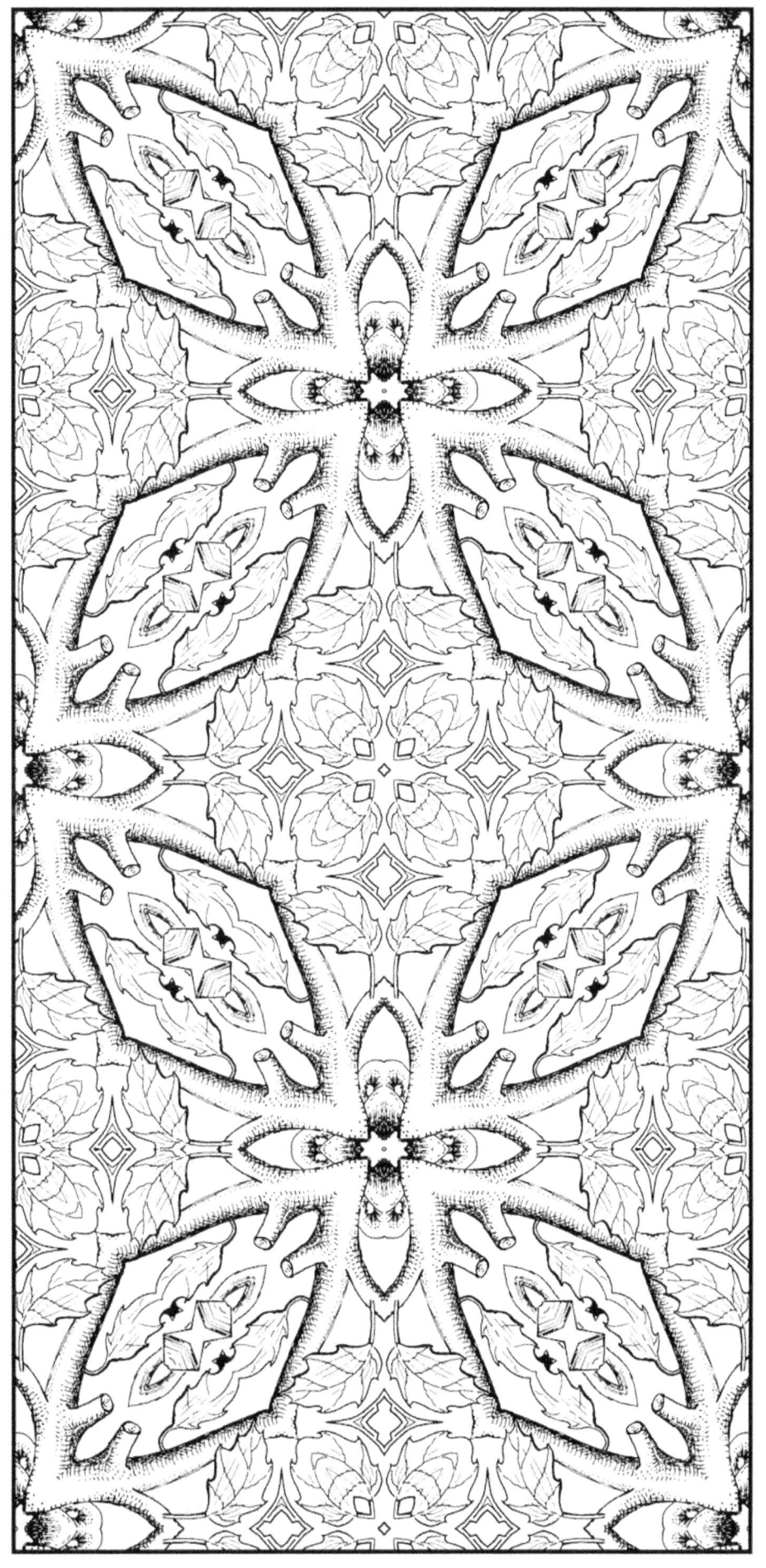

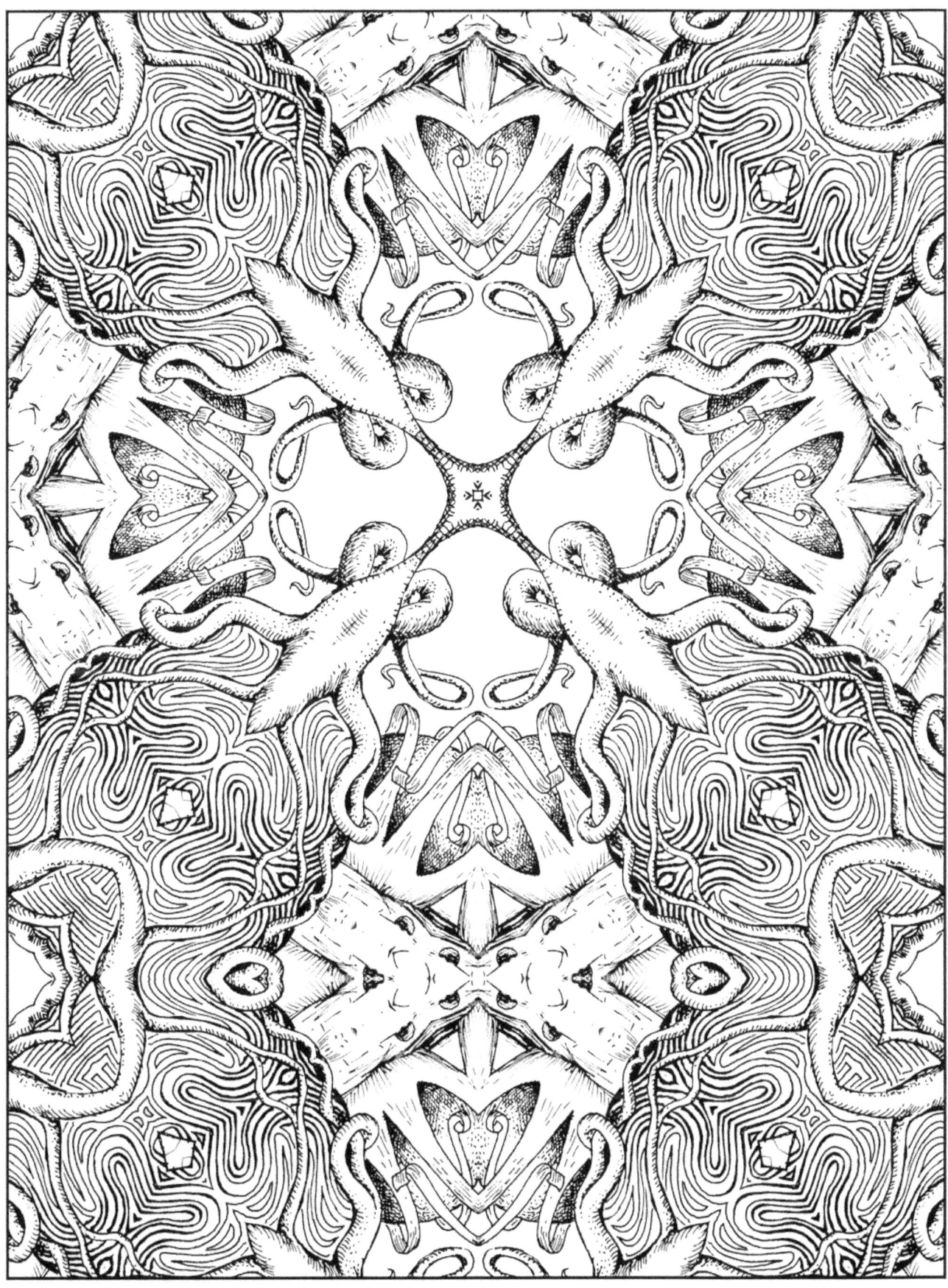

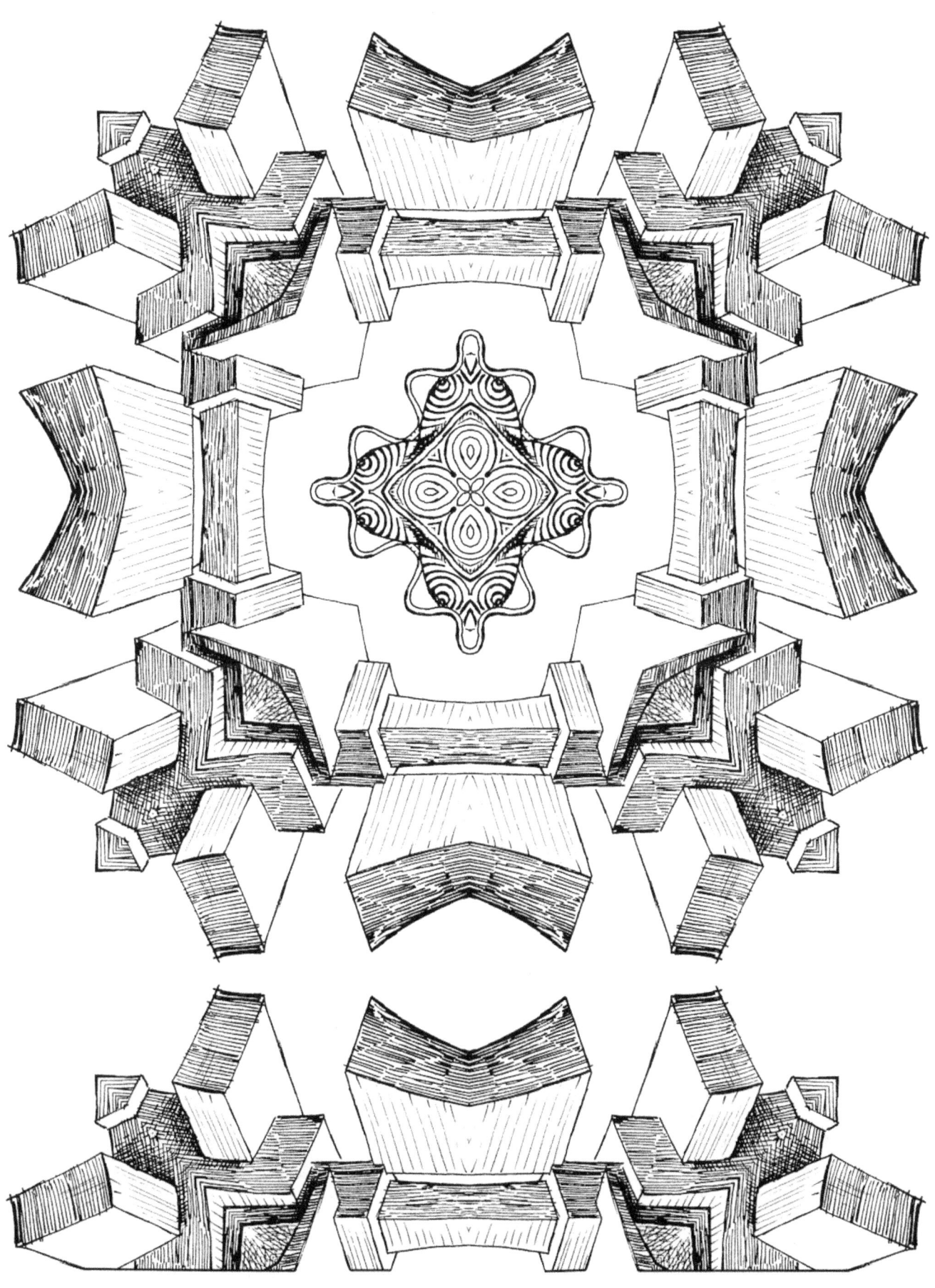

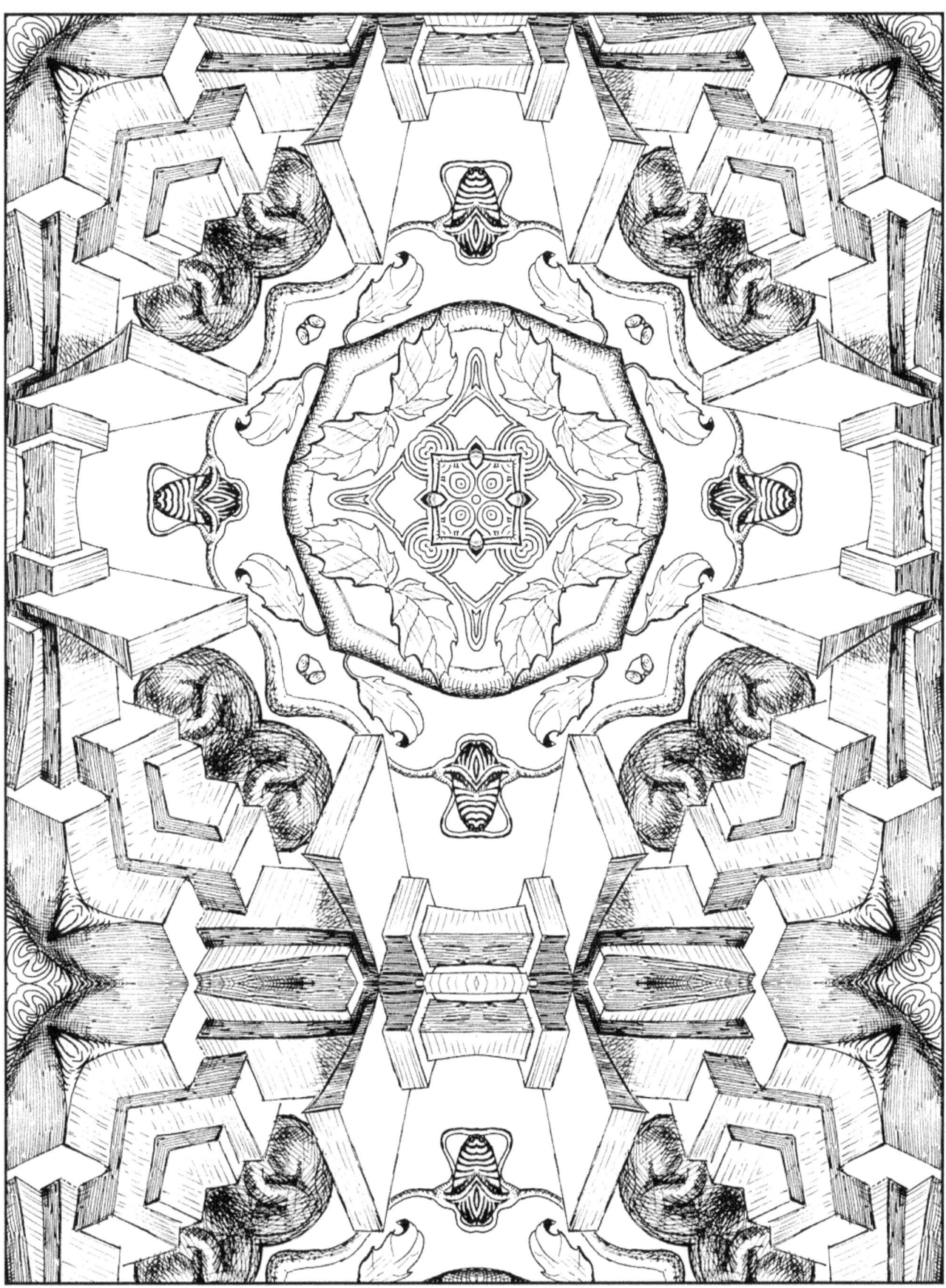

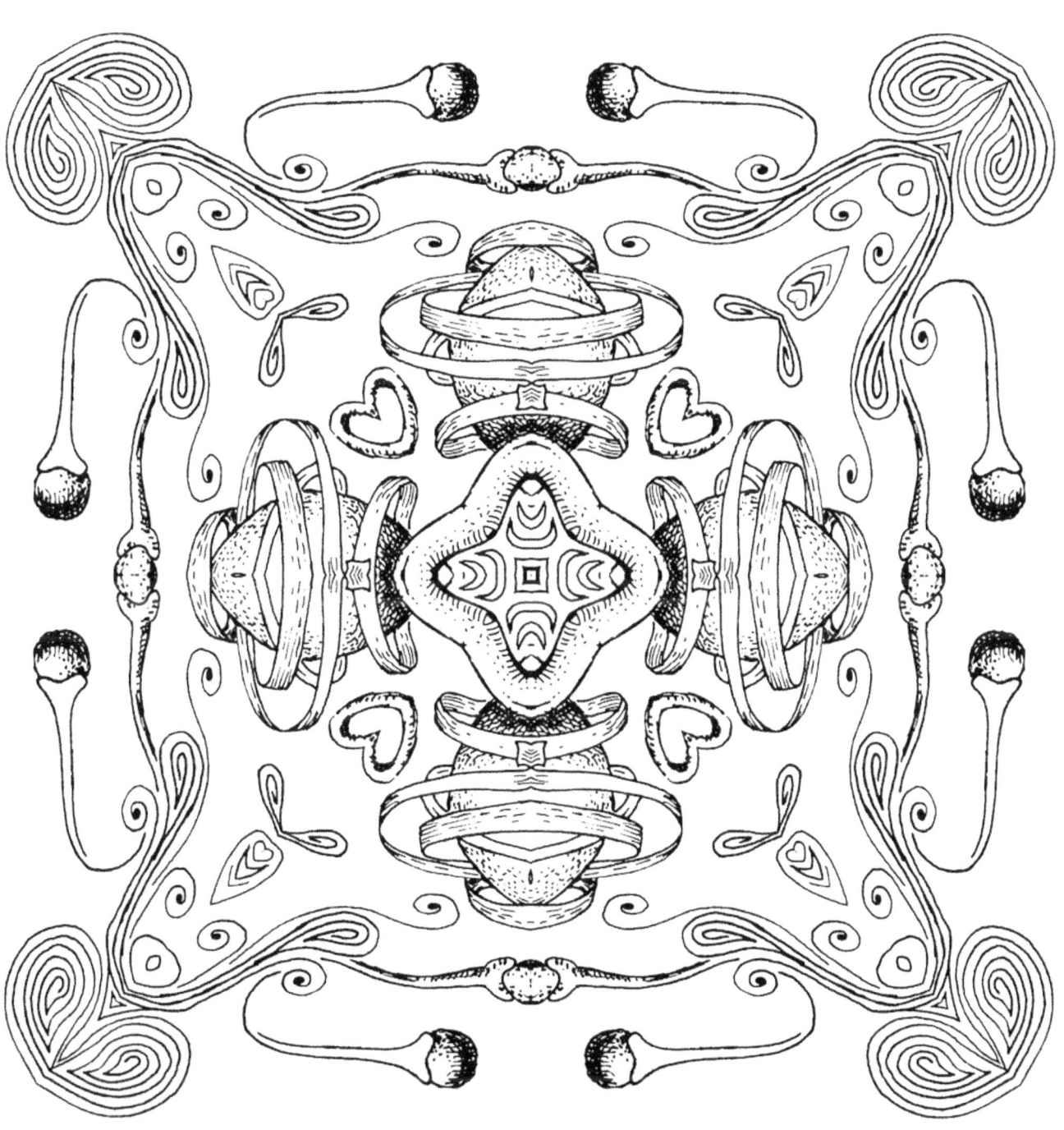

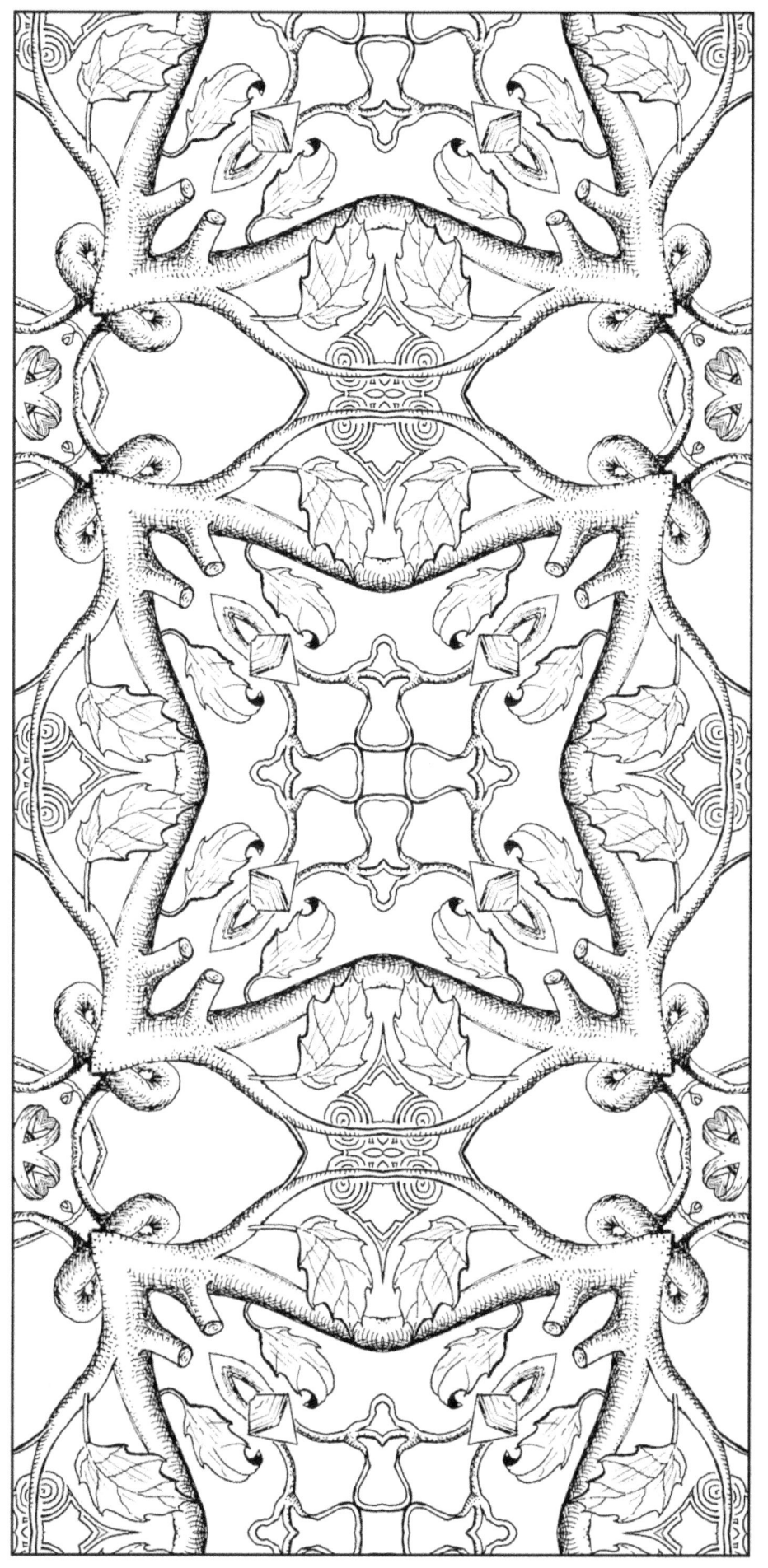

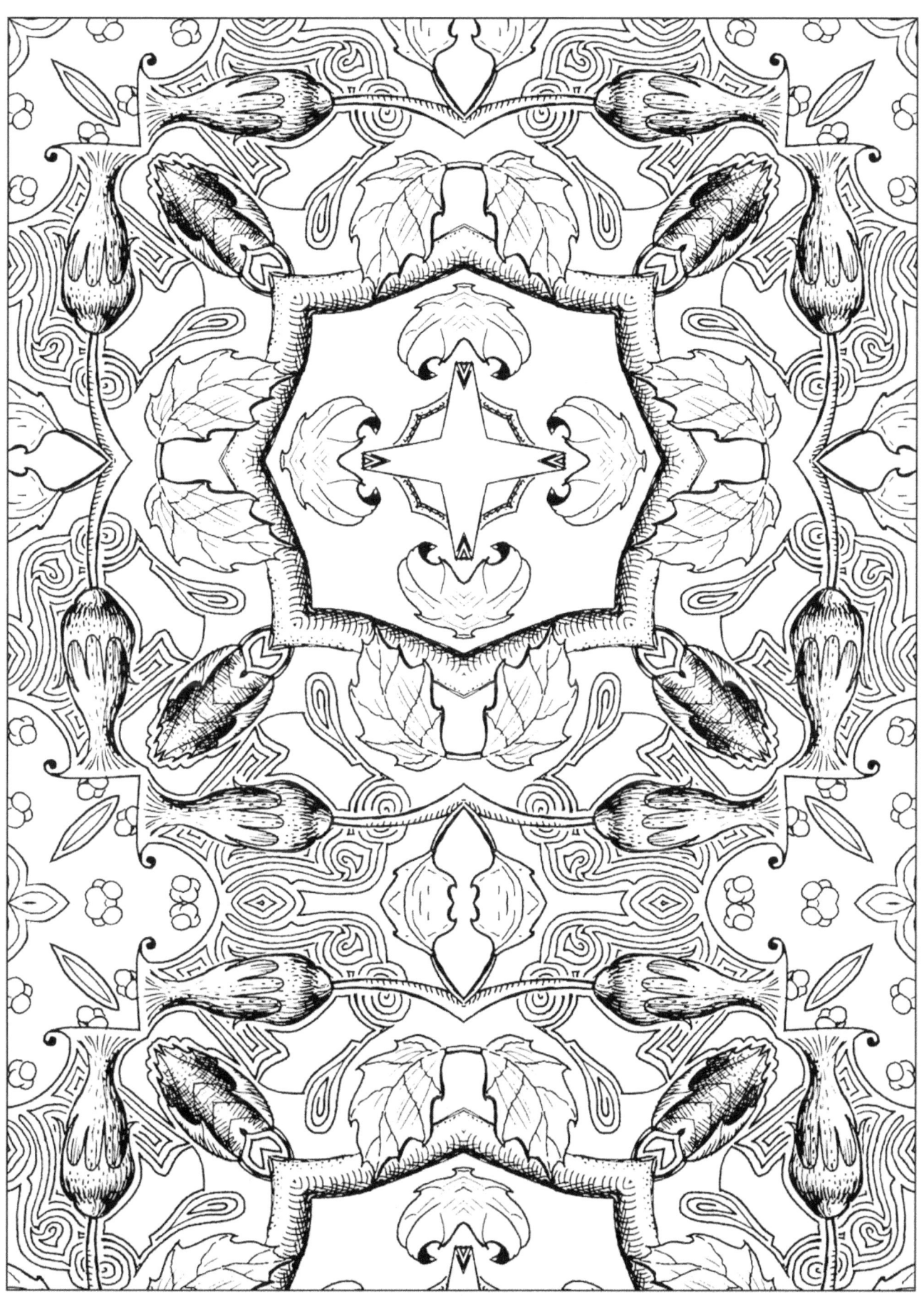

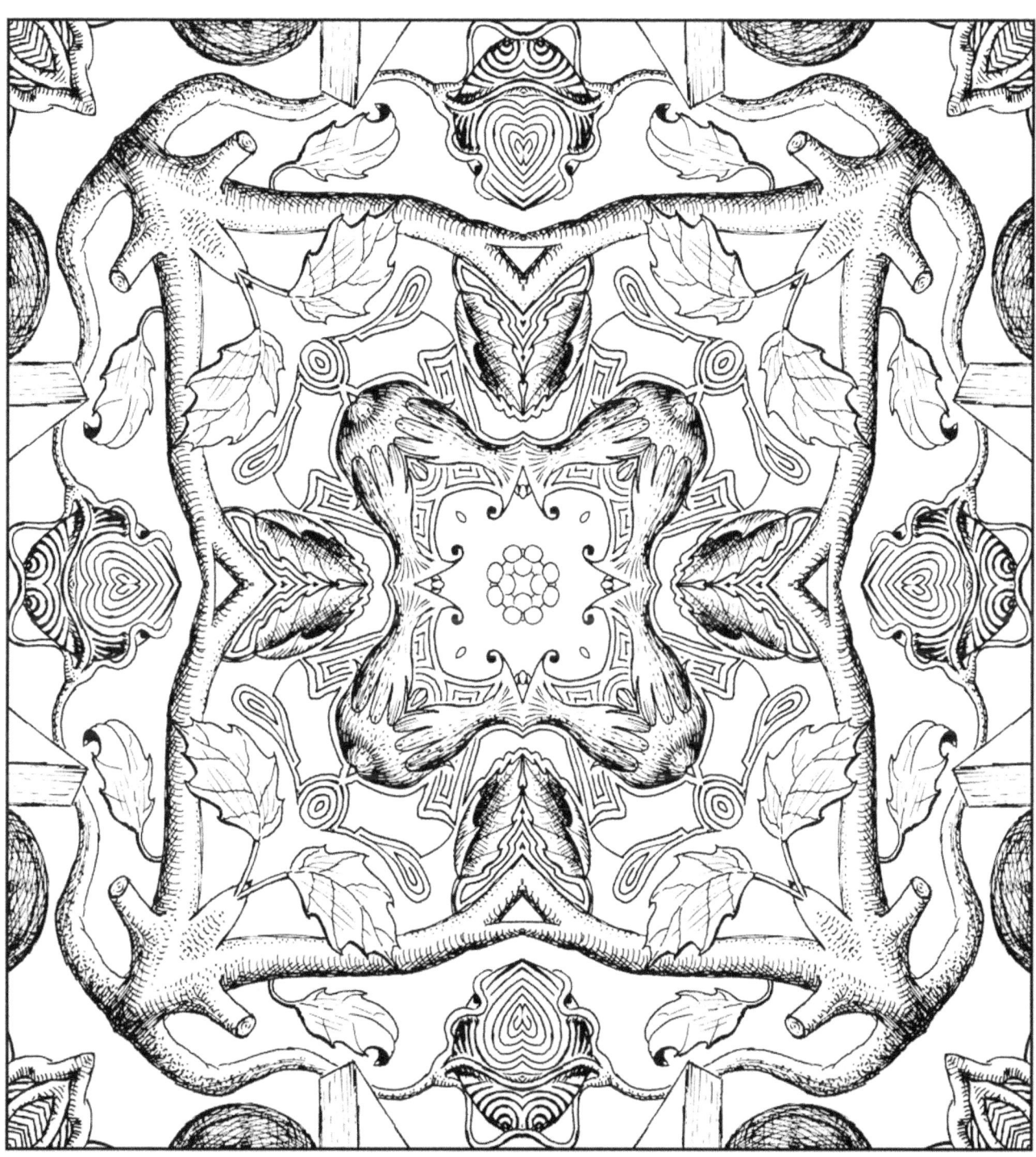

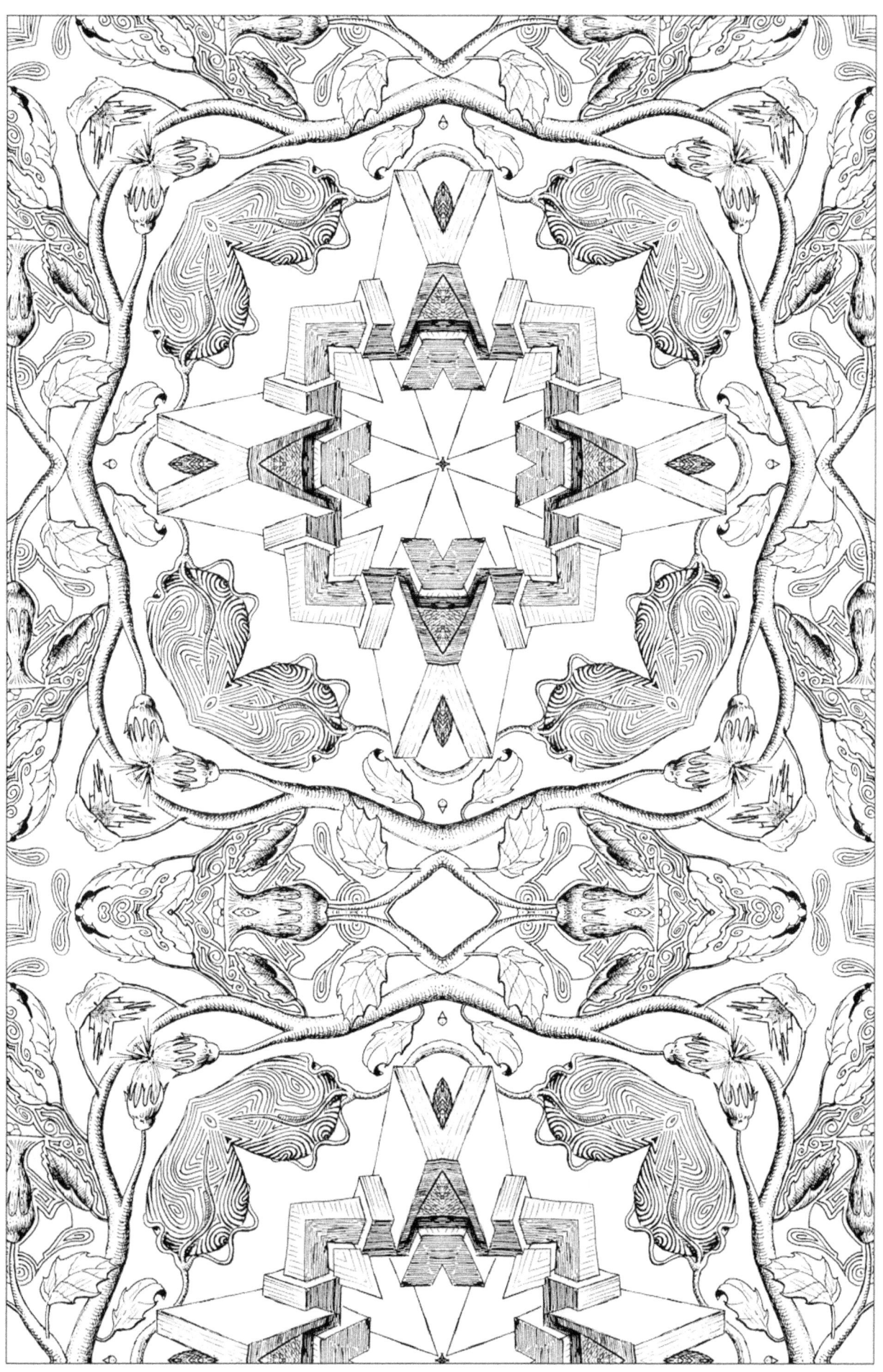

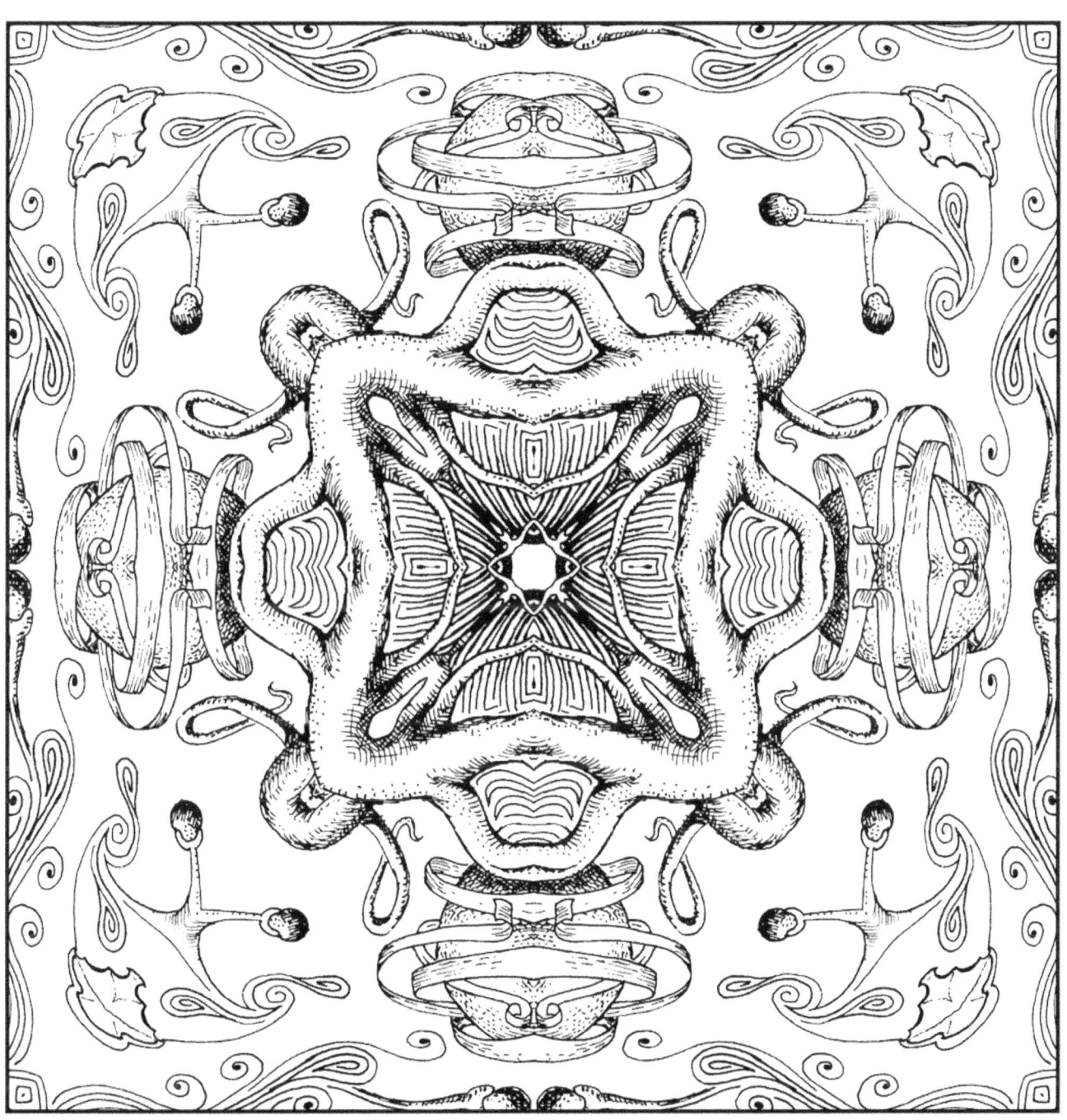

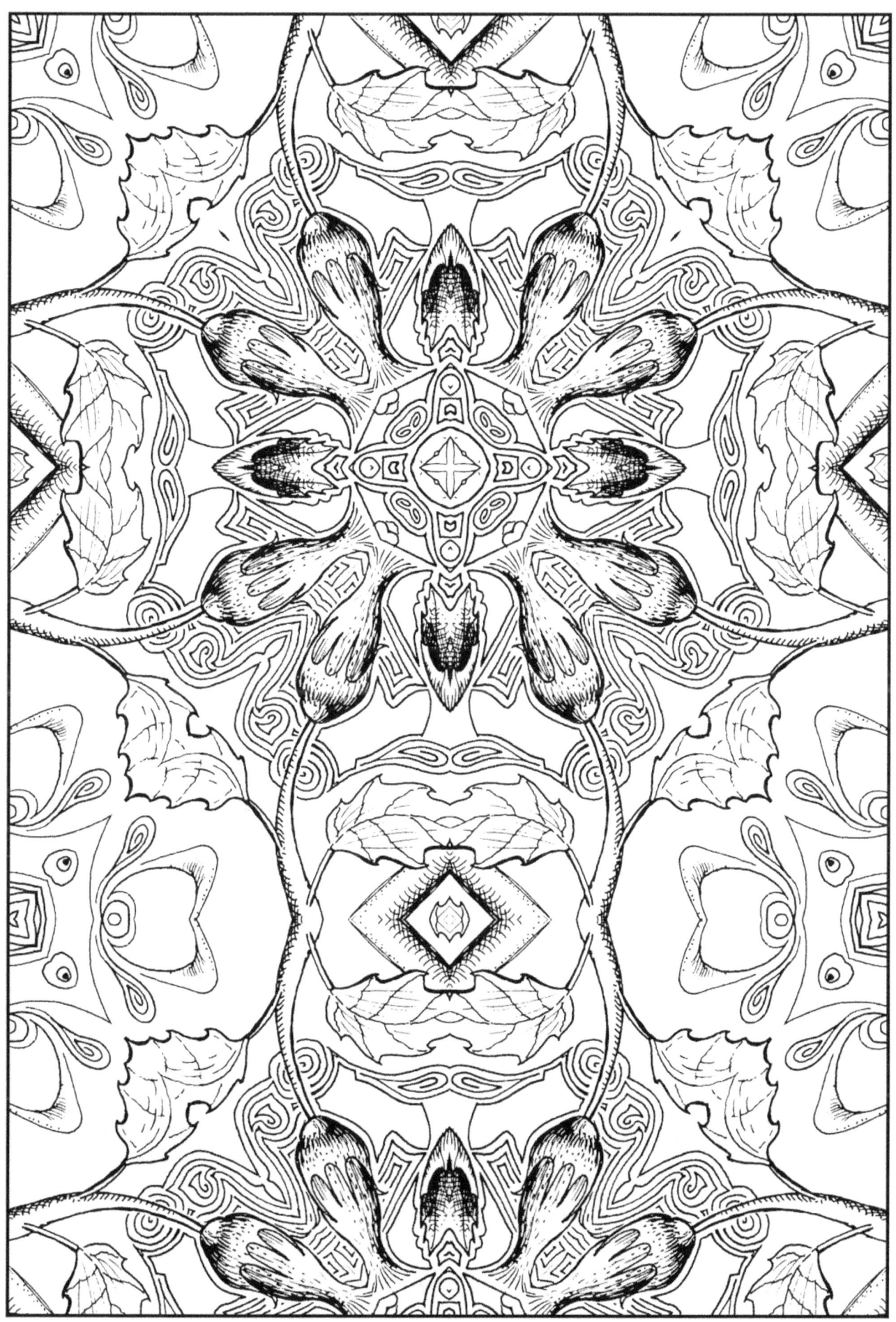

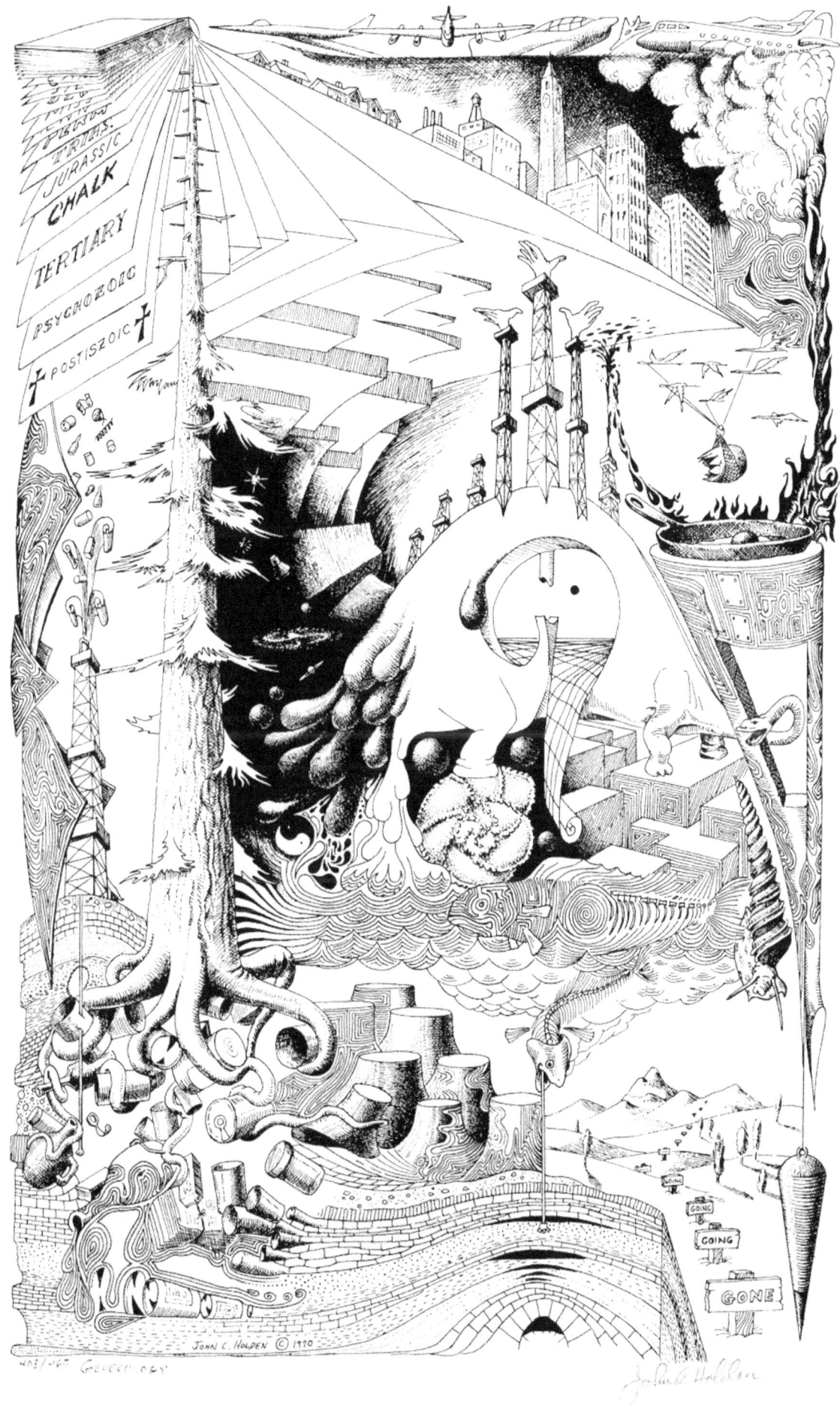

PERM.
TRIAS.
JURASSIC
CHALK
TERTIARY
PSYCHOZOIC
POSTISZOIC

JOHN C. HOLDEN © 1970

GOING
GOING
GONE

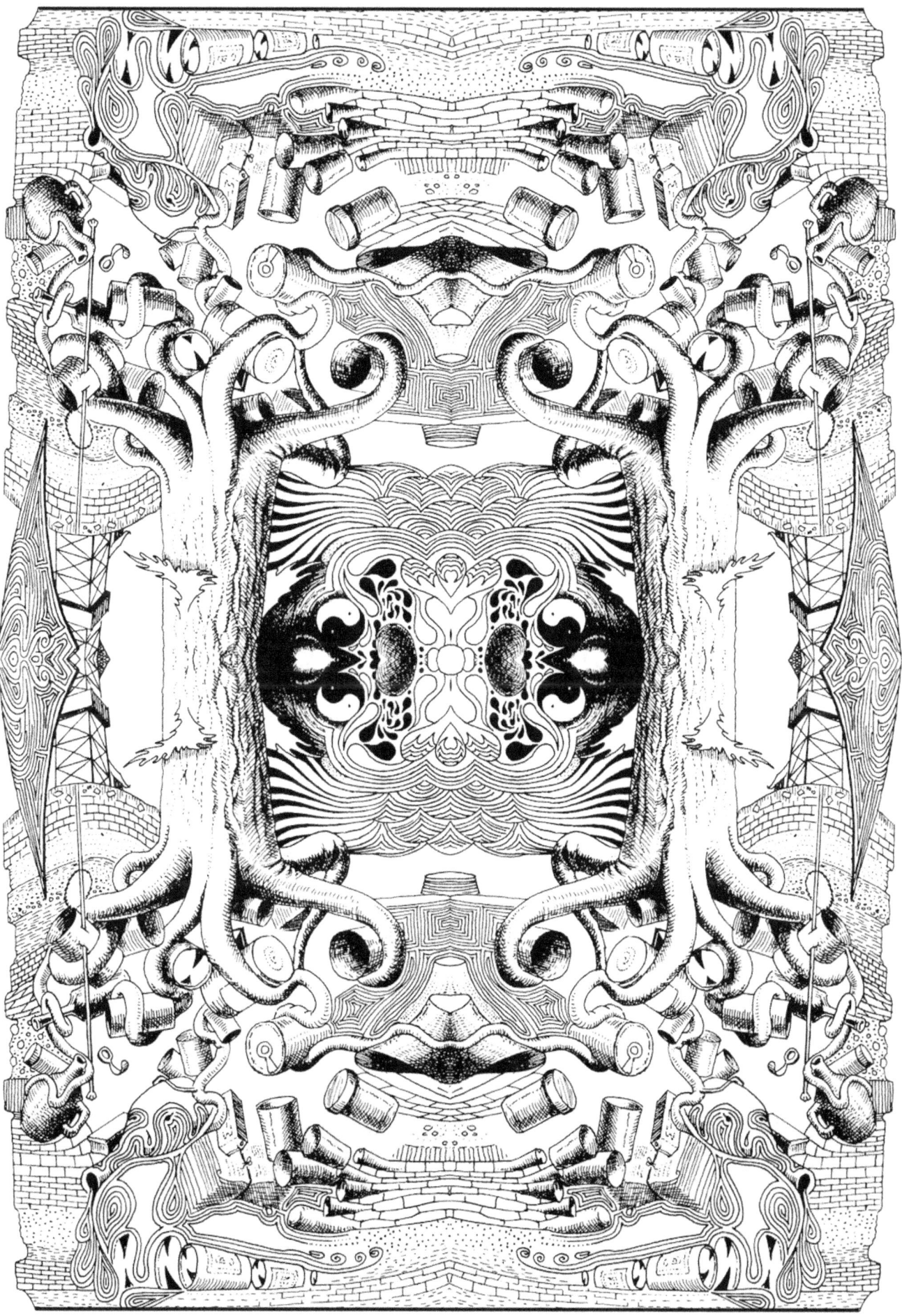

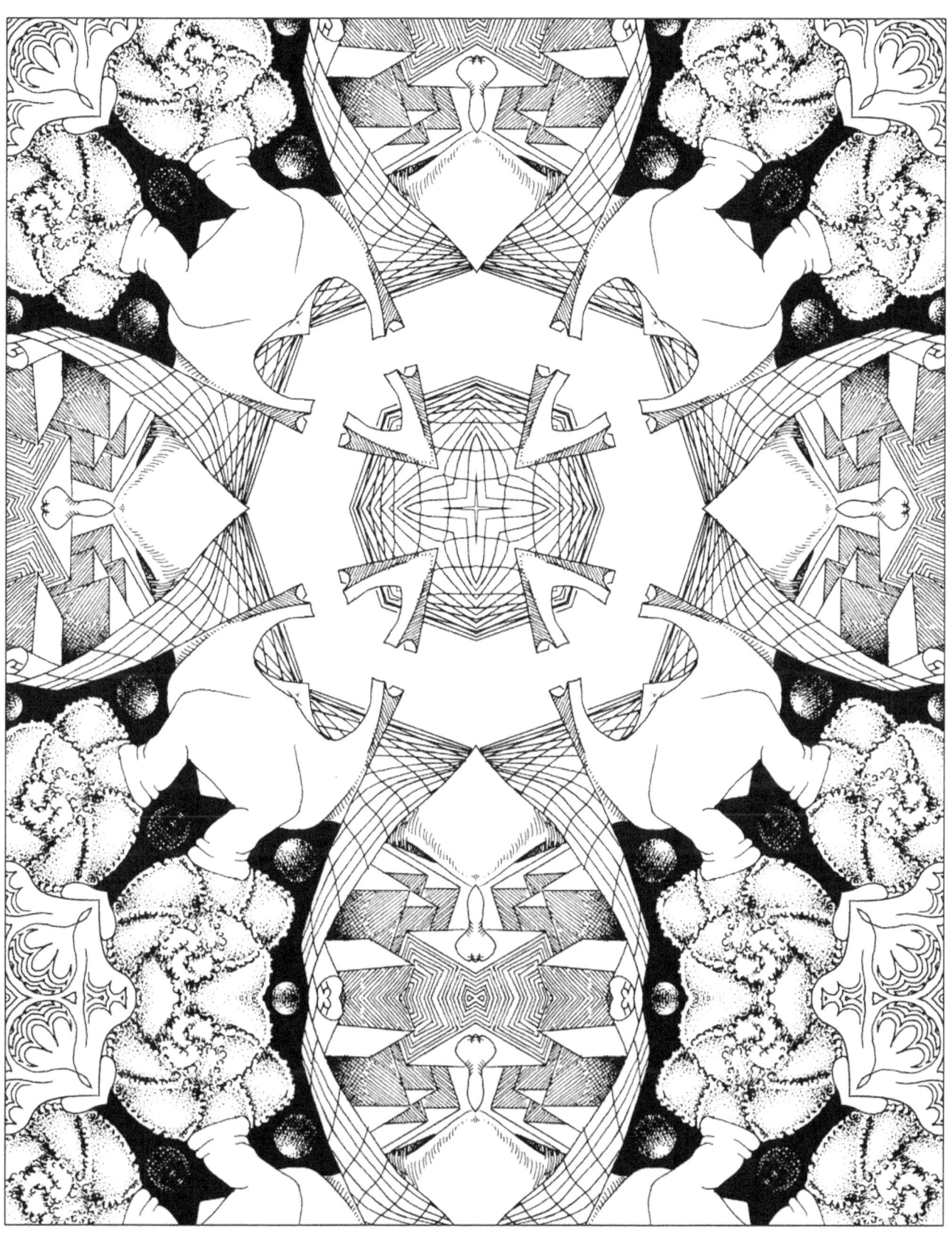

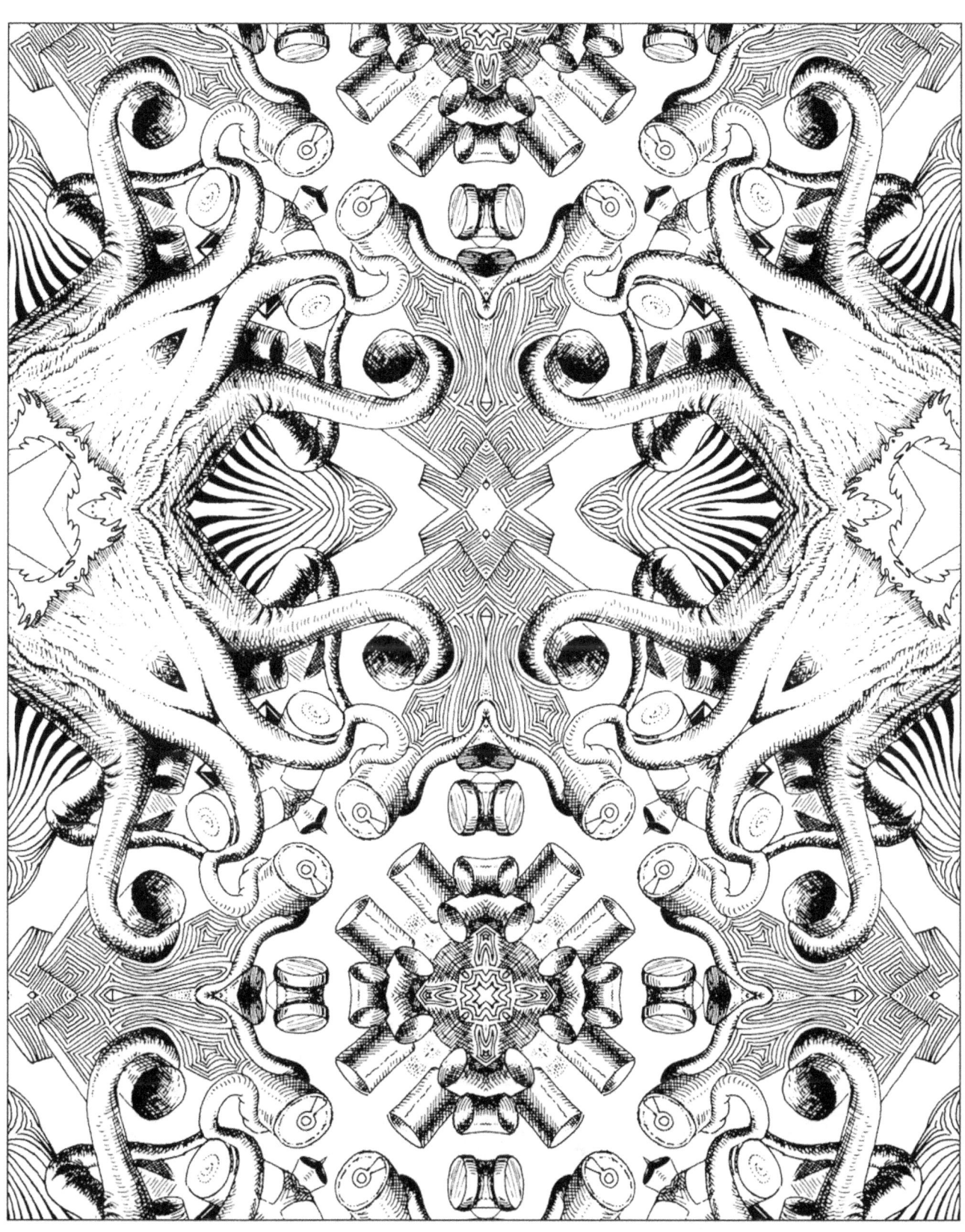

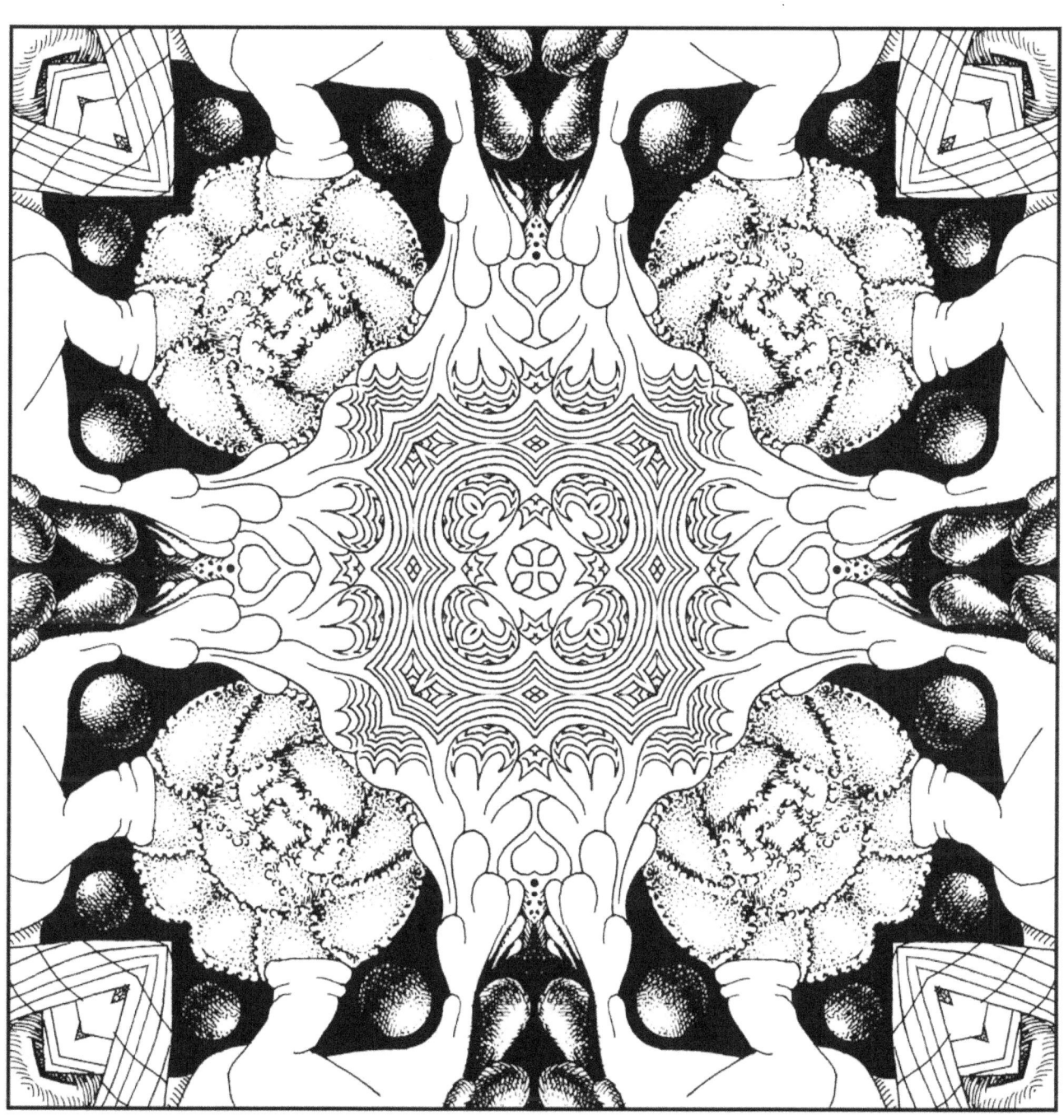

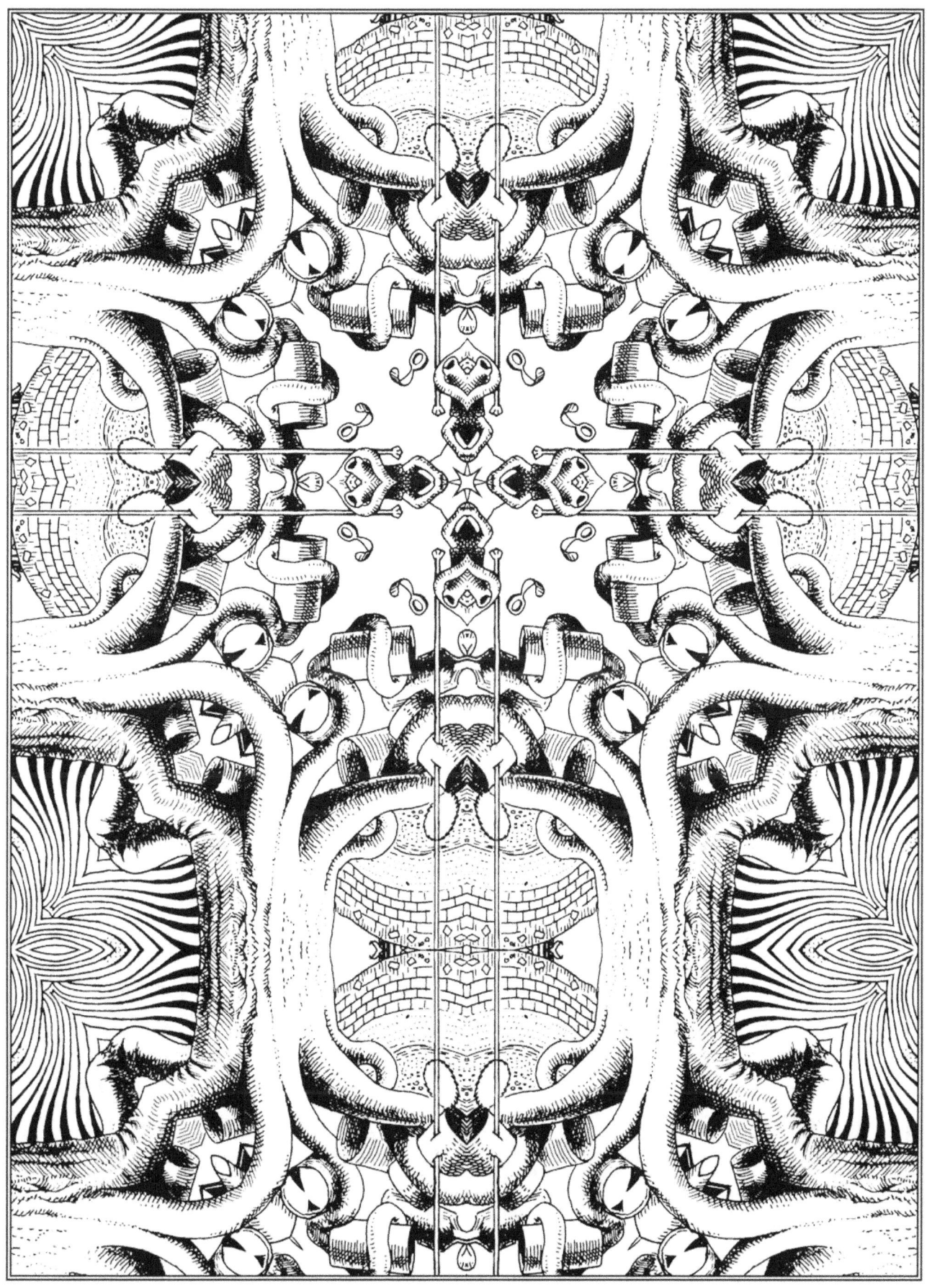

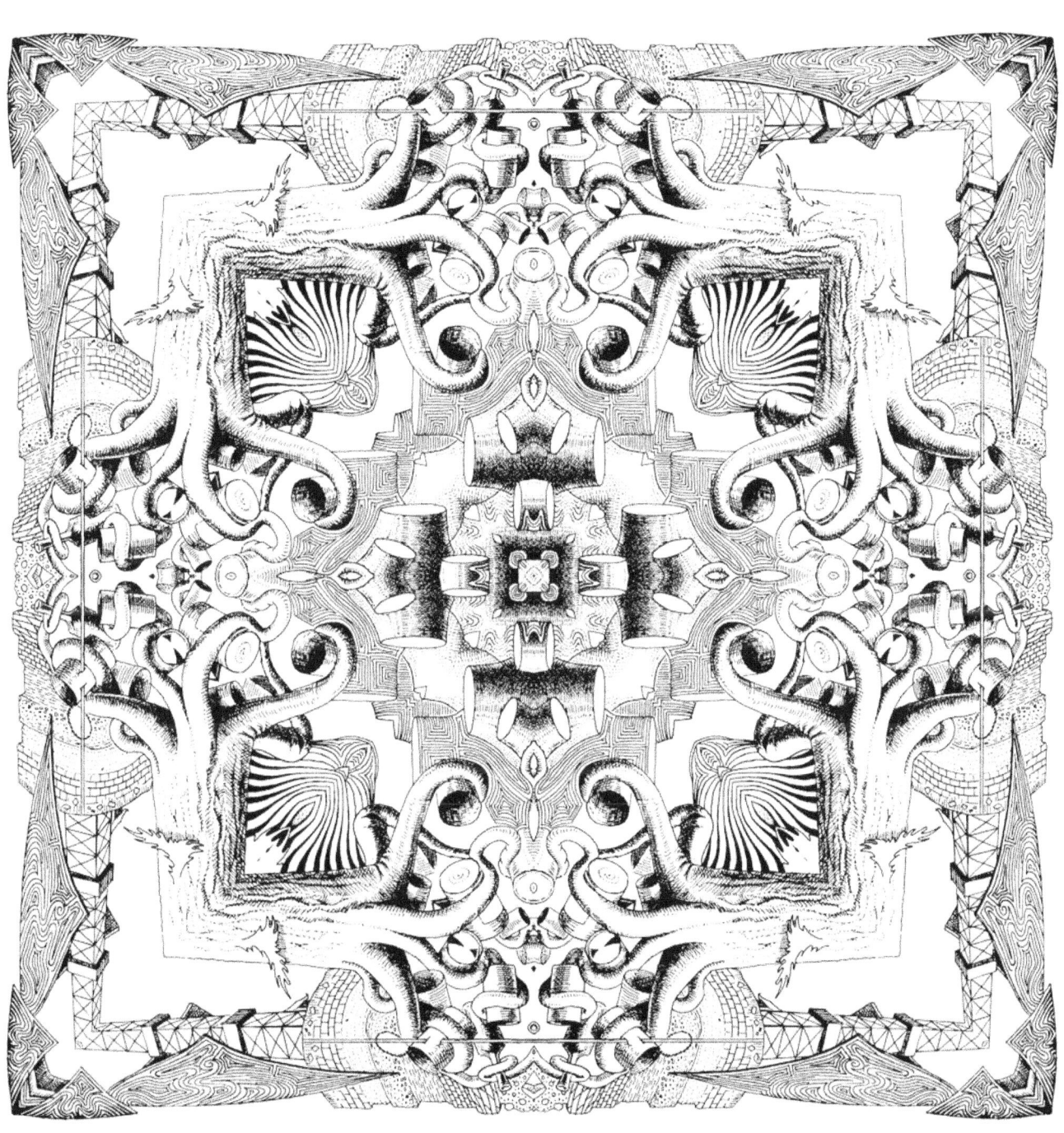

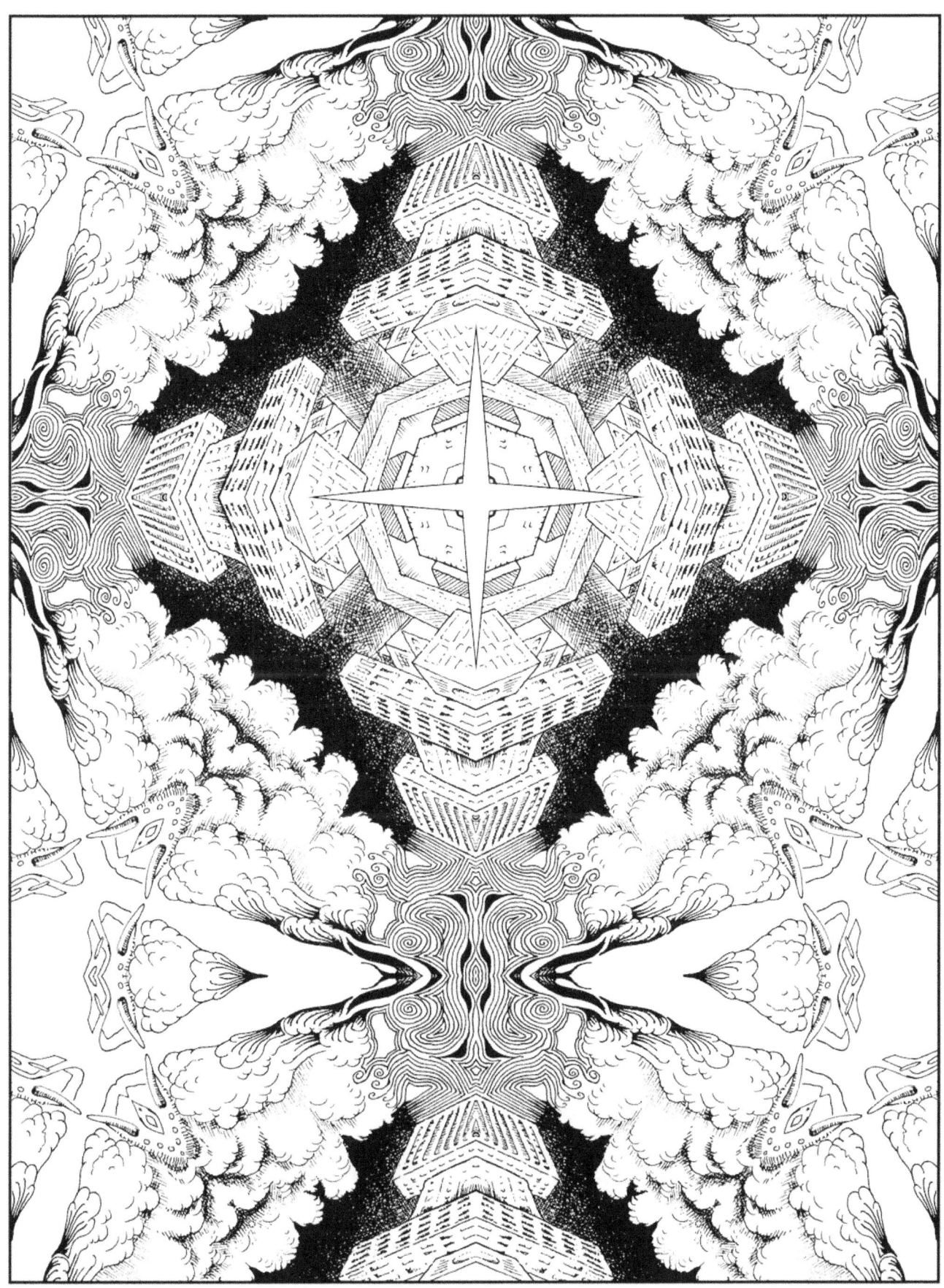

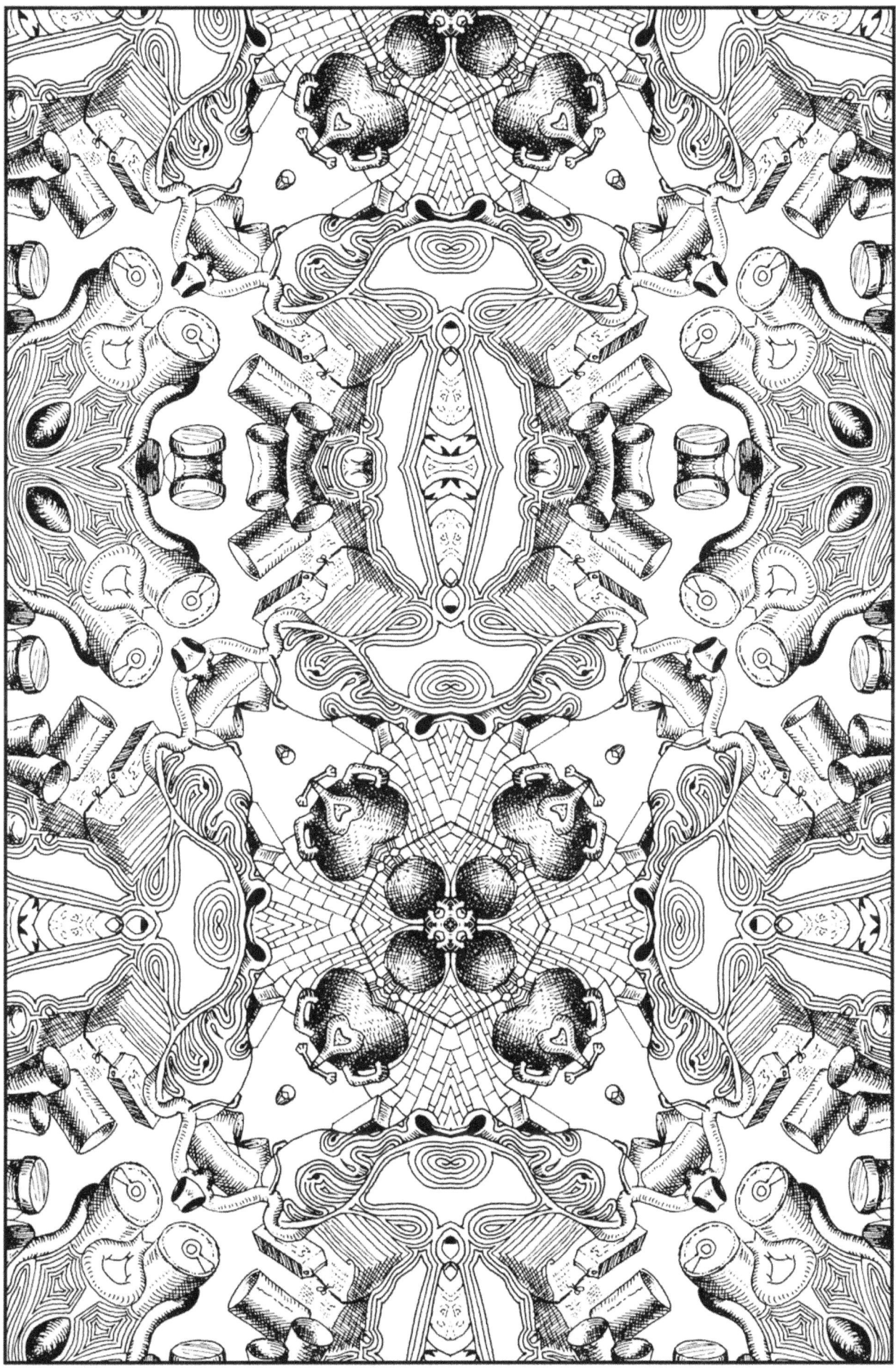

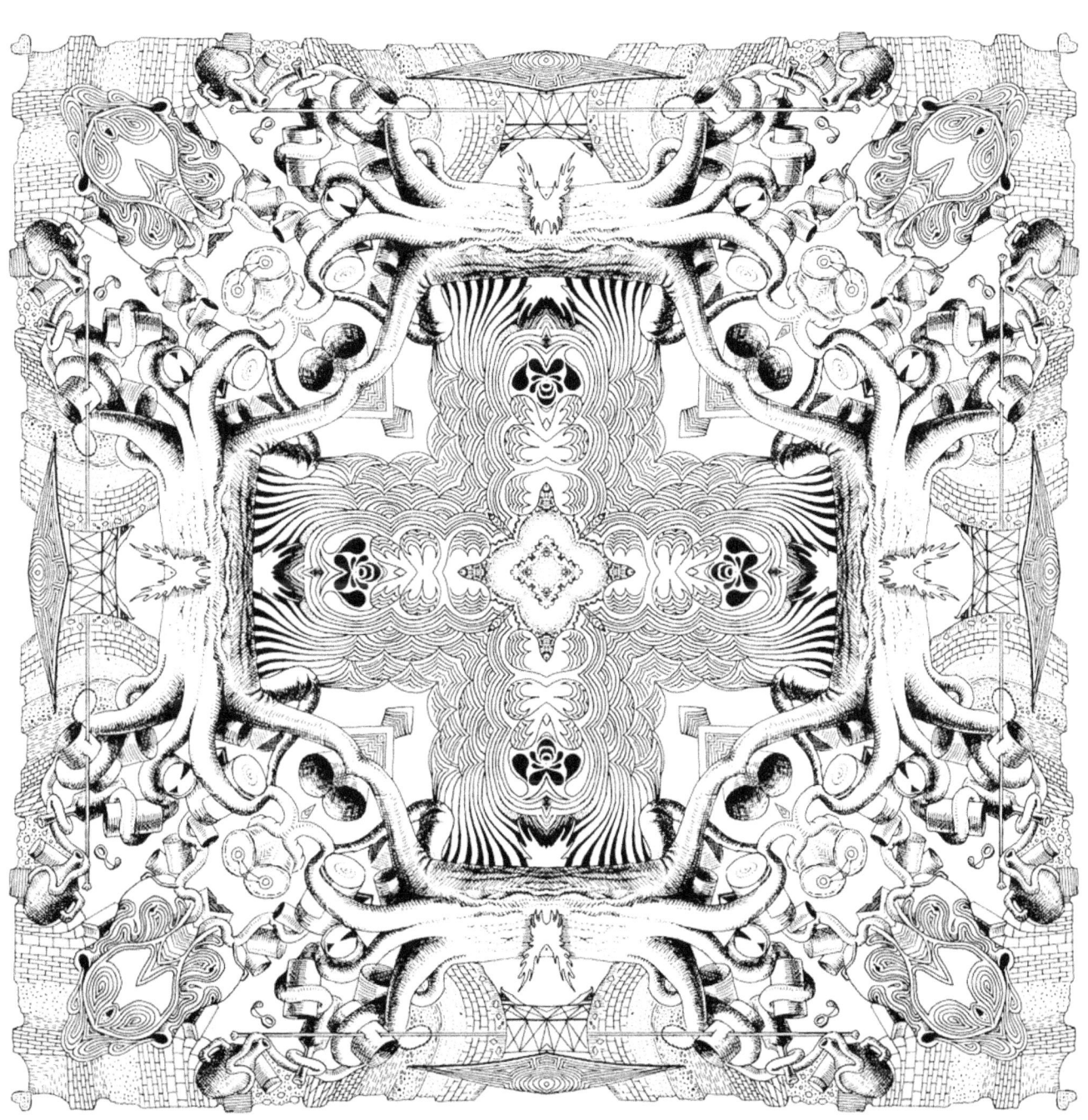

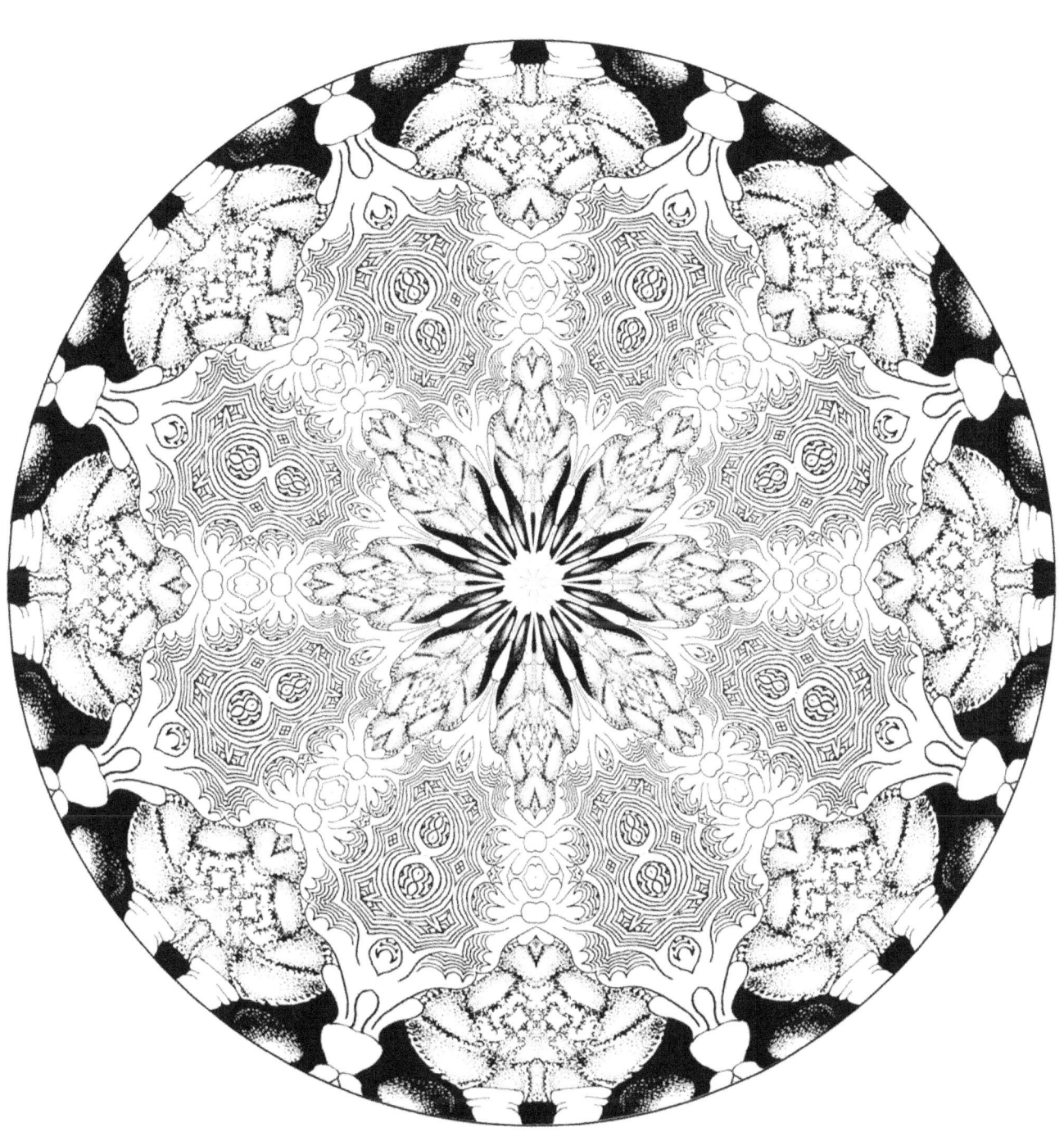

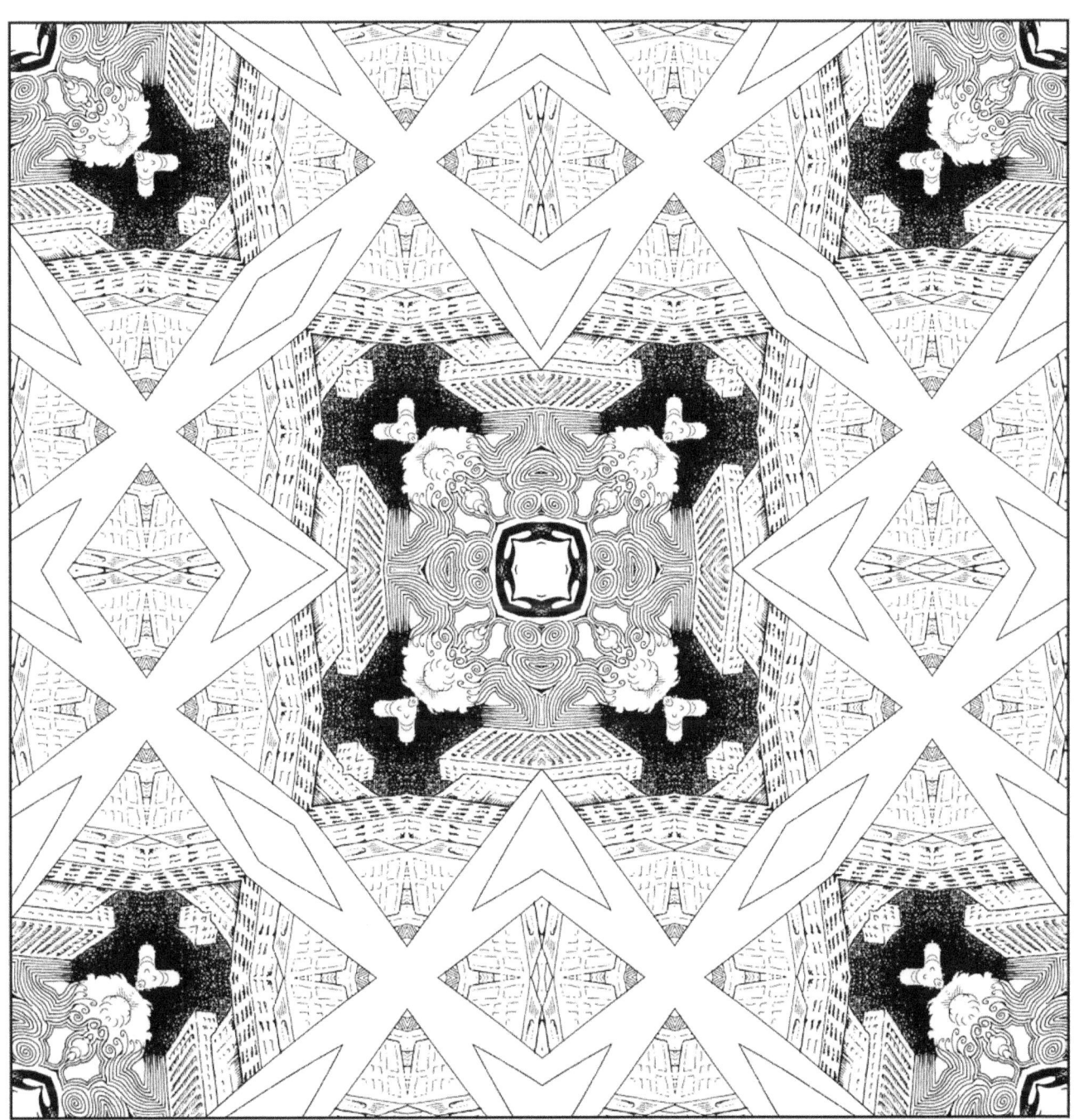

Afterword

This book is the result of a collaboration between Jack (aka John C.) Holden and Gregg Brandly. Jack, armed with pen and paper, is responsible for the drawings. Gregg, equipped with an array of computer programs, produced the patterns from those drawings and the layout for the book.

Jack's drawings were chosen from a series of prints he produced back in a previous millenium. Seven of his smaller prints were used so they wouldn't become too dense when reduced in size as required by the 8.5 x 11 inch page size for the book. The patterns generated from them (or parts thereof) help to open them up to make them more conducive to coloring or, at least, that is the intention. The process of patterning was done with Paint Shop Pro and Filter Forge for the most part.

There is something about Jack's drawing style that seems to lend itself to the various patterning effects and wonderful things happen when his horror vacui and surrealistic sense meet with their own reflection and multiplication. Jack and Gregg find the results agreeable and hope that they have a similar effect on you. Neither of the two are very accomplished in the coloring department, firmly ensconced as they are in the world of black and white, and happily leave that area of endeavor to you.

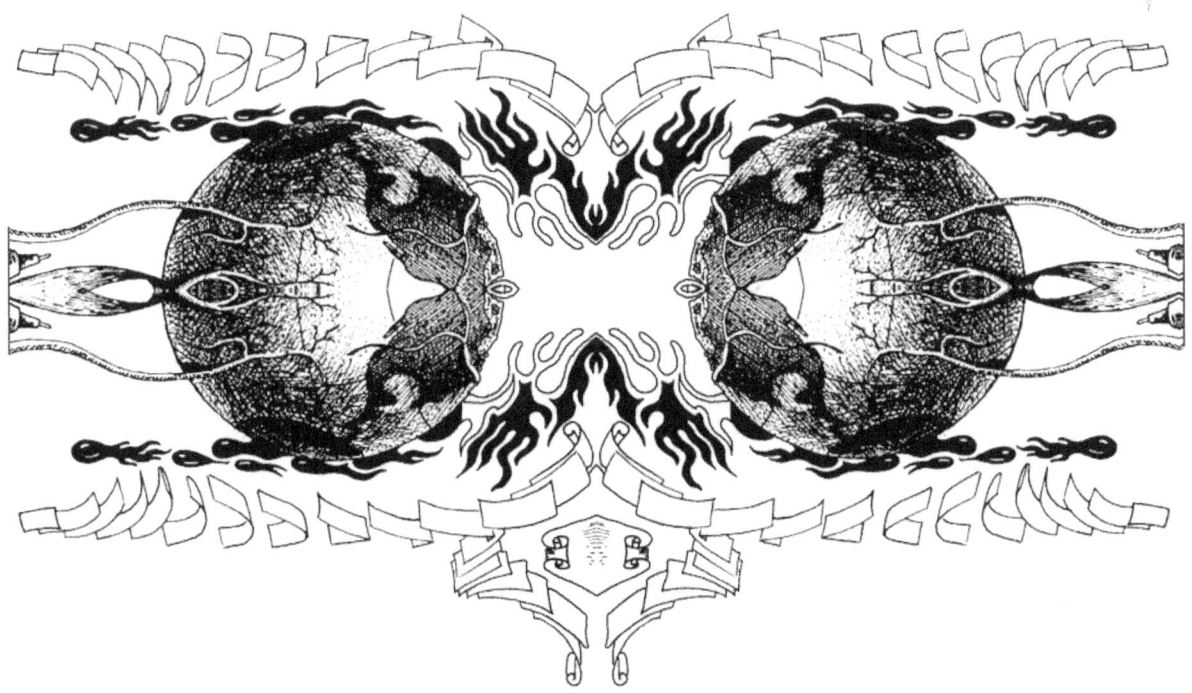

www.ingramcontent.com/pod-product-compliance
Lightning Source LLC
Chambersburg PA
CBHW081123170526
45165CB00008B/2527